A BRIEF HISTORY OF FAYETTEVILLE ARKANSAS

A BRIEF HISTORY OF FAYETTEVILLE · ARKANSAS ·

CHARLES Y. ALISON

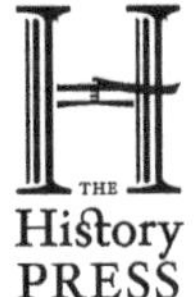

Published by The History Press
Charleston, SC
www.historypress.net

First published 2017

ISBN 9781540215468

Library of Congress Control Number: 2016957612

Notice: The information in this book is true and complete to the best of our knowledge. It is offered without guarantee on the part of the author or The History Press. The author and The History Press disclaim all liability in connection with the use of this book.

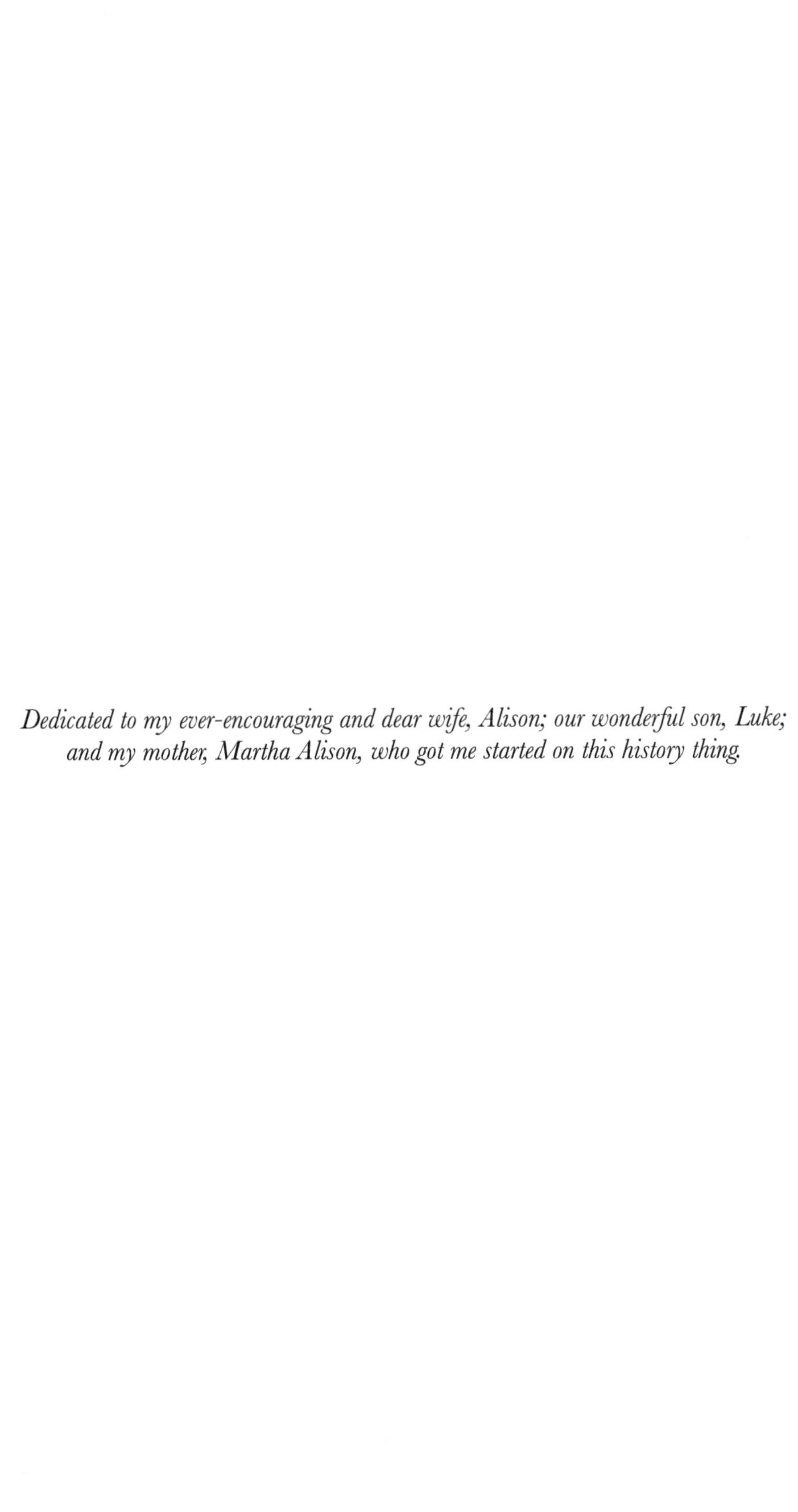

Dedicated to my ever-encouraging and dear wife, Alison; our wonderful son, Luke; and my mother, Martha Alison, who got me started on this history thing.

CONTENTS

PREFACE

Back in 2004, just after I finished a master's degree at the University of Arkansas and had yet to find new employment, John Lewis invited me over to his office at the Bank of Fayetteville. I had pitched the idea of writing a narrative history of Fayetteville, and he wanted to hear more about it. John was always supportive of initiatives that spoke to the quality of life in Fayetteville, and the town's history was one of his own passions.

A narrative history of Fayetteville hadn't been written since the town's centennial in 1928. That history, by William Simeon Campbell, seemed at times to be no less than a gathering of names of nearly every person who had owned a store, broken the law or ridden a pony through town. It's possible that when Campbell wrote his history, not only did everyone in town know everyone else, but also they knew every person who had ever lived in Fayetteville. If I were to write a history, I told John, I wanted to give a sense of the overarching flow of Fayetteville's history, using tales of particular events to illustrate the institutions and culture that have kept the town humming.

As it turned out, I was offered a job at the University of Arkansas before I could get rolling on a history. John died in 2007 of a heart attack, and one of my few regrets is that this brief history of Fayetteville didn't get finished in time for him to read it.

In the intervening years, I collected bits of history here and there, anticipating that I would write something sooner or later. In 2010, Ellen Compton contacted me about putting together a pictorial history of

Fayetteville for Arcadia Publishing. She found photos, and I provided captions for the images. That book came out in 2011. In 2015, The History Press, an imprint of Arcadia, contacted me about this book, part of a series of brief histories of towns all across America.

It is indeed brief by any measure of Fayetteville's history. There are absences in this work. I don't touch on the effect of Fayetteville writers such as Ellen Gilchrist, Charles Finger and Miller Williams and the university's MFA program continue to have on the community. I completely skip over Fayetteville's music scene because a more knowledgeable writer than I should tackle it. Courts and crime, sports, gender issues, class dynamics, politics and many other topics get only glancing mentions. My apologies in advance for missing that one thing you wanted to know.

If nothing else, I hope that those missing pieces coax other writers into researching more of Fayetteville's past as the city approaches its bicentennial in 2028. Fayetteville history during the twentieth century is full of possibilities and barely touched yet by historians.

ACKNOWLEDGEMENTS

Without a doubt, this book would not have happened without the work of many historians who went before me, such as Walter J. Lemke, Lessie Stringfellow Read, William Simeon Campbell and Kent Brown. Whenever I began looking into a historical topic related to Fayetteville, I invariably found that one or more of them had already beaten a well-worn path to the same topic.

Marie Demeroukas of the Shiloh Museum of Ozark History and Joshua Youngblood of the Special Collections Department of the University of Arkansas Libraries were ever helpful in my quest to find photographs to help illustrate this story of Fayetteville.

My thanks also go to Candice Lawrence, my acquisitions editor at The History Press, for luring me into this project, as well as for the line editors who saved me from my own errors.

The directors and executive officers, past and present, of the Washington County Historical Society have encouraged me in chasing odd historical notes and pointing me to sources that I would not have noticed otherwise.

I am extremely indebted to the many friends who are writers and storytellers, wordsmiths and grammar guards. They cannot know how often I've reread their articles and listened to their interviews. They are journalists and history professors and writers of fine literature. And they are inspiring.

On that note about inspiration, I would also have to acknowledge my favorite "historian," the great Arkansas poet John Gould Fletcher, who took a turn into nonfiction to write a history of Arkansas. If there is any lyricism in this book, it's because I read *Arkansas* in my youth and came back to it time and again less for a history than for a writing lesson.

CHAPTER 1
BEFORE FAYETTEVILLE

Before Fayetteville, before Washington County, before there were lines on a map, the land on which Fayetteville now sits was inhabited by Native American tribes. The Quapaws, based along the Mississippi River, traveled up the White River Valley as far as present-day Northwest Arkansas during their hunts. The Caddos to the south also ranged into northern Arkansas. The most frequent visitors and inhabitants of this region, however, were members of the Osage Nation, the Wazhazhes, who centered their autumn and winter habitation along the Missouri River Valley.

As the frozen land turned mushy with thaw and the weather danced between the last cold winds from the northwest plains and the earliest sweeps of warm, rain-filled breezes out of the southwest, the Osages began looking forward to the first full moon of spring. They had a name for each full moon, or the "woman moon." The first full moon of spring was known whimsically as Just-Doing-That Moon:

> *Spring comes to the blackjacks in March, and, roughly, this period is the Osage Just-Doing-That Moon. This is the time of great restlessness in nature; and when they said the Moon Woman was "just doing that," they made a futile attempt to describe her actions. She is like a pampered, temperamental woman who changes from tears and tragic weeping to ecstatic laughter within the hour, during this period of change from winter to summer.*[1]

With spring, the Osages left their winter homes and traveled widely across present-day northern Arkansas, Oklahoma and Kansas, hunting buffalo during the late spring and summer months. A larger period of change came to the Osages after the United States made the Louisiana Purchase and European Americans began moving into region. A treaty with the Osage chiefs in 1808 led to a boundary, known as the Osage Line, being drawn due south from Fort Clark on the Missouri River to the Arkansas River. The Osages agreed to remain west of that imaginary line, a boundary that ran through part of present-day Fayetteville.

In the early 1800s, as the United States began encouraging eastern tribes of Native Americans to move west, several groups of Cherokees traded land in Tennessee for land in northern Arkansas. In moving to the Arkansas Territory, though, they began bumping up against the Osage hunting territory. To allay tensions in 1816, Major William Lovely authorized the purchase of 3 million acres of land west of the Osage Line to create a buffer between the two Native American tribes. It became known as Lovely's Purchase.

Although the buffer eventually helped reduce conflict between the Osages and Cherokees, it also caused confusion regarding where European American immigrants could settle. Were they allowed to settle on the land within Lovely's Purchase? What about areas east of the Osage Line that appeared to not belong to the Osages or the Cherokees?

In 1827, the territorial legislature created a new county called Lovely County. It took in Lovely's Purchase and other land west of the Osage Line. The next year, the current western boundary of Arkansas was created. Lovely County was extinguished in name, if not spirit. The portion of it west of the new territorial line became the Cherokee Nation, while the portion east of the territorial line became Washington County.

CHAPTER 2
WHEN THE TERRITORY WAS YOUNG

On a late afternoon in 1819, a herd of buffalo grazed on thickets of grass sweeping across a broad, open expanse of prairie, hemmed in by mountains on the south side of what is now Fayetteville. Grasses such as bluestem, switchgrass, broomsedge and ticklegrass covered the lowlands. Thick woods of hickory, ash, pecan, oak and cedar climbed the surrounding mountainsides. Rutted buffalo paths led in every direction from one brackish salt lick to the next. Across the open valley, a scraggy line of trees—box elder, catalpa, bois d'arc, sweet gum and cottonwood—bordered the banks of a creek. At the eastern end of the valley, the creek joined the West Fork of the White River.

Sitting near the confluence of that creek and river was a hunter and trapper named Frank Pierce. Like the French trappers before him, Pierce had followed the wending bends of the White River upstream, looking for game. Earlier that year, Congress had created the Arkansas Territory, splitting it off from the Missouri Territory to the north. Still mostly an unsettled wilderness, the northwestern corner of this new territory teemed with wildlife: elk, black bear, beaver, fox, wolf, deer, panther, bobcat and the aforementioned buffalo. Looking out across the grassland, Pierce could see the herd of buffalo and quietly sought a point of advantage to take a shot at them. As he maneuvered for a good position and took aim, though, "he saw a band of Indians. He lowered his gun without firing, dropped under the bank and retired for the night under friendly shelter of a large elm."[2]

The next morning, Pierce struck out for the Illinois River to the west. Early in the morning, he crossed the creek valley and hiked over a rise of land that is the present site of the Fayetteville Square. He continued westerly until he hit the Illinois River and then followed it south to the Arkansas River, where he turned downstream toward the Mississippi River and the territorial capital of Arkansas Post, some 350 miles away.

Pierce is the first known European American to visit what is now Fayetteville, but he was probably only one of many European visitors to the region. French trappers combed the waters of the *Rivière Blanche*, hunting beaver, fox and bear, while the region was part of Louisiana, a French colony from 1682 to 1763. These hunters shipped their hides and bear fat down the Mississippi River to New Orleans. A few early maps also note two European families living on the upper reaches of the White River, perhaps as high as the confluence of the East, Middle and West Forks of the White, although the scale of the maps is too ambiguous to know for sure. One site is noted as "Plantation de Guillaume" on French maps (or "Williams" on English maps), and a second establishment is designated "Etabt. [des] Futenap" (or "Futenah" on the English maps).[3]

In 1828, the year the region was opened to white settlement, Frank Pierce came back to the broad valley and the creek now known as Town Branch, and he settled near the spot where, nine years earlier, he had spent the night, bivouacked in hiding from the band of Native Americans.[4]

Ahead of Pierce were seven families, already staking homesteads. James McGarrah and Mary Rowell McGarrah were the first to arrive with their family, although it is highly likely that James McGarrah had visited the area before, scouting, hunting or trapping. He and his wife grew up in South Carolina, where he served as a colonel for the South Carolina militia during the War of 1812. They came to Northeast Arkansas as early as 1809, moving up the White River Valley. When Washington County was opened to European American settlement, the McGarrah family settled near Big Spring, claiming acreage north of present-day Spring Street to Maple Street and west to present-day College Avenue. They built a log cabin near the current intersection of Conner and Trent Streets. Their son, George, took over the family homestead and became known during his lifetime as Fayetteville's first resident.

The quick movement of settlers into the community and its central location to the county, which initially included present-day Benton County and parts of Madison and Carroll Counties, led the state to designate the community as the county seat of Washington County. Although the community was initially known as Washington Court House, the U.S. postmaster asked within the first year that the name be changed because another town in Arkansas was already named Washington. The town's three commissioners chose the name of Fayetteville because two of them hailed from Fayetteville, Tennessee. The county commissioners also appropriated $49.75 to build a log courthouse.

Initially, Fayetteville settlers rode to Cane Hill and Evansville for supplies, food and dry goods. Sometime in 1829, though, Washington Wilson and his wife built a home on one corner of the square and began operating a dry goods business out of it.

Earlier that same year, a sixteen-year-old girl named Charlotte Fine moved from Tennessee to Arkansas with her parents. They came in two wagons, the first a large "prairie schooner" driven by four horses and the second a two-horse wagon. Their route was typical of many immigrants, following the Arkansas River Valley as far as Van Buren and then turning north along the military road, coming in by way of Billingsley near present-day Hogeye. In early March, just as the lingering snows melted, the family settled about seven miles south of Fayetteville along the banks of the West Fork of the White. There were no neighbors, no visitors and no community yet save the budding town of Fayetteville, nearly an hour's ride away.

Lonely for social contact, Charlotte "felt herself very fortunate when she received a ticket to a ball to be given by the young gentlemen of Fayetteville on the 4th of July, 1829." Her mother and father drove her into town the morning of the fourth, and she recalled seeing no other house in the seven-mile span. Dancing commenced at 2:00 p.m. on the puncheon floor of the newly built courthouse, a twenty-foot-square log building that stood at about the intersection of present-day Center Street and Block Avenue. "A splendid supper was served at Byrneside's Tavern, and each young gentleman was taxed $1.50 for supper for himself and partner." A dozen young ladies attended the dance, most of them town girls, and a like number of young gentlemen. "They danced some square dances, but mostly the old Virginia eight-handed reels, which required no one to prompt. She danced her first set with Thos. Wilson, to whom she married on the 6th of the following September, 1829."[5]

Things move pretty fast in Fayetteville. From its beginning, Fayetteville drew people from across the county and the region into town for commerce, for civic needs and for entertainment and social repartee.

Among the institutions providing civic cohesiveness, social opportunities and spiritual growth were the churches developed during the period prior to the Civil War. The earliest organization of churches began in 1830. The town had only seventy-five residents, but that didn't stop a few residents from organizing to start the Cumberland Presbyterian Church. Reverend Andrew Buchanan of Cane Hill came up to Fayetteville to meet with interested residents in a blacksmith shop owned by John Lewis on East Center Street. Other churches soon took shape as more residents of differing denominations moved to the town.

The Methodist Episcopal Church South was organized at the home of Lodowic Brodie in 1834. In 1848, two churches were founded: the Episcopal Church, established by Reverend W.C. Stout, and the Christian Church, founded by Robert Graham. The next year, Catholic congregants began meeting together, although formal organization of a church didn't happen until 1878. A Missionary Baptist Church was organized by Reverend John Mayes in 1858.

Building a Network of Roads

Early transportation was difficult and generally followed the traces and paths created by the Native Americans who lived in and traveled through the region before the territorial days. The earliest roads were funded by Congress to provide easier movement of military troops and increase safety. In 1833, the Arkansas Territorial Assembly petitioned the U.S. Congress to pay for the clearing of a road across northern Arkansas, to run from Jackson in Lawrence County through the towns of Liberty and Fayetteville and then south to Fort Smith. By the next year, Lieutenant Richard D.C. Collins was in Arkansas surveying a route, and construction began the next year after crops were laid by.

In May 1834, the G Company of the U.S. Dragoons passed through Fayetteville on a march along the military road from Jefferson Barracks in Bloomington, Iowa, to Fort Gibson, Indian Territory. The death of Charles Gatliff and the desertion of Christopher Bench were noted at Fayetteville. Among the officers of G Company passing through were Lieutenant Jefferson Davis, later the president of the Confederate States of America, and Captain Nathan Boone, the youngest son of Daniel Boone. One of the dragoons reported:

> *The next morning we passed through a smart little town called Fayetteville, and encamped in the evening upon a beautiful spot about three miles distant from it. The face of the country had now become much improved, and instead of the patches of scrub oaks through which we had been traveling, we now met with heavy forests of large oaks, elms and pekaun trees, and now and then a clump of pines that retained their beautiful green appearance throughout the winter, and relieved the more somber hue of their companions.*[6]

Along with churches, commerce began on the square. Other frame buildings went up around the square to provide dry goods, millinery products and saddle and tack, as well as professional services of lawyers and doctors. In 1834, Congress authorized the county commissioners to sell 160 acres of land to pay the cost of building a proper courthouse. James Byrnside purchased the lot at the south end of what is now Block Avenue on the Fayetteville Square in 1836 and erected a large log house that soon became a well-known tavern and hotel that survived until the Civil War. The *Arkansas Advocate* advertised the sale of the land and described the region:

> *The town is admirably situated, on a beautiful eminence, on the dividing line between the waters of the Illinoi* [sic] *and White Rivers. On the south and east, the blue hills and mountains, with intervening prairies, present themselves as far as the eye can reach; and on the southwest, there is much prairie land, of excellent quality. The growth of the adjacent forest is oak, hickory, ash, mulberry, walnut, cherry, black locust, paw-paw, spice-wood, and the largest and most delicious grape in the world.*[7]

President Andrew Jackson issued a patent for the land of the original town on February 27, 1835. It was described as the south half of the northeast quarter and north half of the southeast quarter of Section 16, Township 16, Range 30 West. In easier terms to understand, this is the land bounded by what are now College Avenue on the east, Gregg Avenue on the west, Dickson Street on the north and South Street on the south. Soon after, the city was surveyed into lots by Charles McClelland, the deputy county surveyor, and a survey team that included John West, William McGarrah, James Parr, John Smallman and A. Mankins. All of the lots except the center of the square were auctioned off by A. Whinnery between 1835 and 1837, raising $6,339 in the course of 169 sales, the money being used for erection of a courthouse and clerk's office. After the 160 acres of land sold, the rough-hewn log courthouse and puncheon floor on which Charlotte Fine had danced were replaced by a brick courthouse at the center of the square, finished by 1837.

Early Statesmen Arrive

Two early Fayetteville immigrants—David Walker and Archibald Yell—arrived in Fayetteville during the 1830s. They were a contrast in style, politics and personality. Walker grew up in Kentucky and attended school briefly, learning more by studying under an uncle and then reading law on his own. In 1830, at the age of twenty-four, he struck out for the Arkansas Territory, finding his way west to Fayetteville, where he set up shop as a lawyer and was elected prosecuting attorney in 1833. Two years later, Archibald Yell arrived in Fayetteville by appointment of Andrew Jackson as circuit judge. He was about thirty-eight years old. He had been raised in Tennessee and while still a teen threw in his lot with Jackson, fighting in the Creek and Seminole Wars, as well as the War of 1812, in which he received due notice from Jackson during the Battle of New Orleans.

Walker was reserved in judgment, thoughtful and a Whig. Yell was bigger than life, charismatic and a Democrat of the Jacksonian strain.

Walker resigned his position as prosecutor after winning a seat in the territorial legislature in 1835. The next year, he served as a member of the convention that wrote the state's first constitution. Meanwhile, Yell settled into the dispensation of justice on the frontier, in one case ordering a man to stand in the pillory on the Fayetteville Square. In another instance, an accused man refused to come to court. Yell found the man at a local saloon and dragged him out of his cups, commanding him, "God damn you. Come into court and answer to your name and to the indictments against you!" The man had little choice but comply.

Upon Arkansas statehood in 1836, Yell ran for Congress.[8] He would have preferred to run for governor, but the legislature included a residency requirement that specifically prevented Yell from running. He won the Congressional race handily and then ran for governor in 1838, again winning easily. Walker, meanwhile, was elected to the Arkansas Senate in 1840.

Yell and Walker often partnered in financial ventures, including a good deal of land speculation. In 1836, for instance, the two along with William

Haile proposed a new port town on the Arkansas River. They named it Ozark and offered lots for sale. During the 1838 General Assembly, Walker and a group of men formed the Fayetteville and Ozark Turnpike Company, which was incorporated by the state legislature. The company sold shares at fifty dollars each to fund construction of a road between Fayetteville and Ozark, which made the latter town a more convenient stop for travelers along the Arkansas River bound for Fayetteville. Today, that road is known as the "Pig Trail."[9]

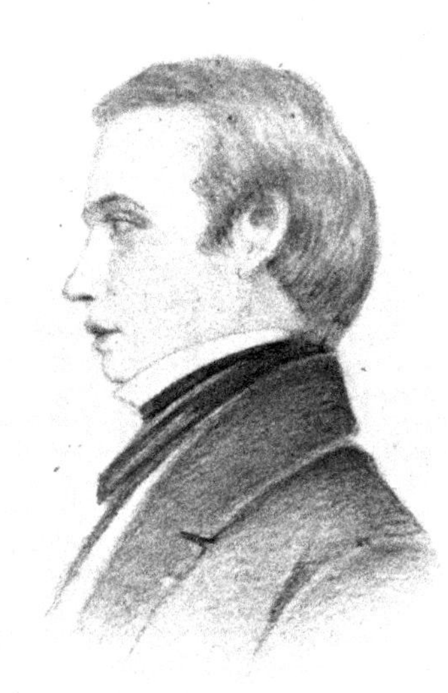

A pencil drawing of David Walker from 1830, about the time he moved to Fayetteville and began practice as an attorney. *Courtesy Washington County Historical Society.*

Both men purchased large farms in the Fayetteville area. Yell bought significant holdings on the south side of Fayetteville and built a four-room Greek Revival house atop a small knoll overlooking the farmlands. He named it Waxhaws in honor of the Carolina region where his friend and future president James K. Polk was born and reared. The house was razed in 1963, but the Washington County Historical Society saved Yell's law office from the site and moved it to the grounds of Headquarters House.

Walker bought one thousand acres of farmland in the valley of the White River east of Fayetteville.[10] He also built an early brick house in Fayetteville on Center Street. He later sold it to merchant Stephen K. Stone and his wife, Amanda. Still standing, it became known as the Walker-Stone House and was purchased in 2016 by the Fayetteville Advertising and Promotion Commission.

Their close friendship and financial entanglements, however, didn't prevent them from finding each other on opposite sides of a political race. In 1844, the Whigs of Arkansas nominated Walker as their candidate for Congress. The Democrats nominated Yell. They canvassed the state together. The partisan state newspapers could be vicious in their attempts to belittle the opposing party's candidate, but on the stump, Walker and Yell avoided personal invective. Nevertheless, personality played a deeply important role in the result. Walker told a story on himself. At one speaking

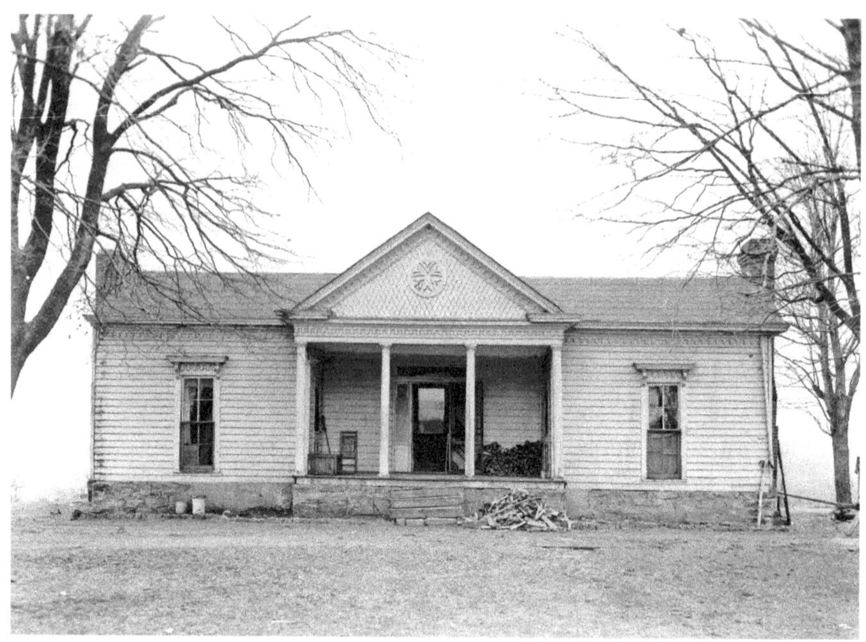

Archibald Yell built this Neoclassical house on the south side of Fayetteville and named it Waxhaws in honor of the South Carolina region where his friend President James K. Polk was born and reared. The house, probably built in the early 1840s, stood atop a hill overlooking Yell's extensive farm. The house was razed in the 1960s, and the Fayetteville Senior Center is now located nearby. *Author's collection.*

engagement during the canvass, Yell and Walker arrived and found a shooting match underway. Yell purchased a chance, shot straight and won the prize, which he donated to the most needy widow in the neighborhood; then he bought a jug of whiskey for the crowd. Walker suffered through this in quiet because he did not abide games of chance or alcohol. Later in the campaign, though, Walker thought Yell would have his comeuppance. The two candidates joined a camp meeting, but before Walker knew it, Yell was leading the singers in their hymns and shouting the loudest clarion call from the "amen corner." Walker remarked, "You can't beat such a man as that. He is all things to all men, and all men believe in him. He is as popular with psalm-singers as with those who take their dram and shoot for beef."[11]

In fact, Yell won the election, capturing 59 percent of the vote. He carried thirty-six counties to Walker's ten. Yell's seeming victory, however, proved a first step toward a struggle that would end his life. While attending Polk's inauguration as president, Polk dispatched Yell to Texas to persuade the Texans to allow annexation of the republic as another state. Yell was successful

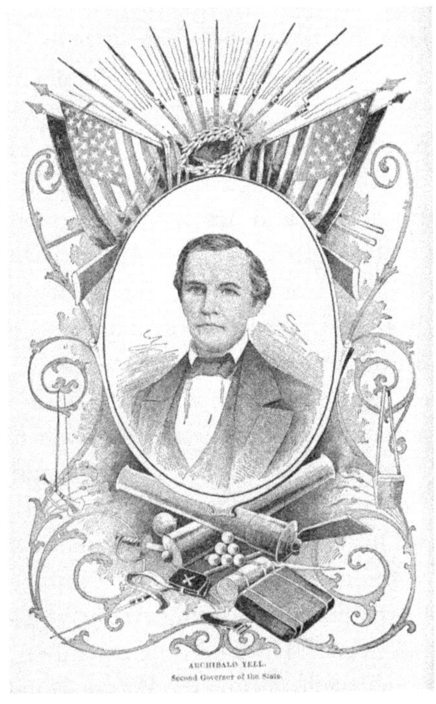

Archibald Yell, the state's first representative to Congress and its second governor, came to Fayetteville in 1835 as the territorial circuit judge. He died in 1847 at the Battle of Buena Vista during the Mexican-American War. *Author's collection.*

in large part, although Sam Houston only agreed not to actively oppose annexation. In October 1845, the Texans overwhelmingly approved annexation. Still awaiting his own Congressional swearing-in ceremony, Yell wrote to President Polk to advocate a war with Mexico to settle the boundary of Texas and make clear America's military strength. He declared that he would not leave his seat in Congress without the pleasure of voting for a war. In May 1846, the war came. General Zachary Taylor's forces on the Texas side of the Rio Grande were attacked, and Polk issued a proclamation of war with Mexico. By June 18, Yell was back in Little Rock, enlisting as a private in the Arkansas Volunteers. He was soon elected colonel of the Arkansas troops, and by August 28, his troops arrived in San Antonio, where they were attached to an expedition heading to the Mexican state of Chihuahua. They were eventually dispatched to the town of Saltillo and remained in that area for the next two months, hearing rumors that Mexican general Antonio López de Santa Anna was planning an attack.

After skirmishes between Santa Anna's forces and Taylor's troops on February 22, 1847, the Battle of Buena Vista commenced the morning of February 23. Yell's regiment was placed on the extreme left of the American front. Mexican artillery bombarded the left, forcing the Americans back, but Yell rallied part of his troops to face Mexican lancers advancing quickly into the American lines. He charged into Mexican troops and was killed almost immediately by the pierces of lances to his head and chest. After Santa Anna's troops withdrew, American troops found Yell and buried him near the battlefield. President Polk called him a "brave and a good man" who was "among the best friends I had on earth."[12] Some months later, his family brought his body back to Fayetteville and reinterred him at Waxhaws. When Evergreen Cemetery was opened after the Civil War, the bodies of Yell and his family were moved to it. David Walker wrote the text for Yell's tombstone.

Walker, though he did not have Yell's penchant for war, lived to serve Fayetteville and Arkansas for another three decades. In 1848, he was elected associate justice of the Arkansas Supreme Court, serving until 1855. In 1861, he was elected president of the state convention to consider secession and led Unionists in avoiding secession when the convention first met in March. After the fall of Fort Sumter, though, he could not prevent the rush among delegates to vote for secession and in the end joined them, afterward accepting appointment as a colonel assigned to a Confederate military court. Following the war, he was reelected as chief justice of the state Supreme Court and served until a new state constitution was approved in 1868.[13]

On the centennial of American independence, Walker represented Arkansas at the Centennial Exhibition in Philadelphia, where he addressed the exhibition, praising Arkansas, lauding its history and expanding on its resources.[14] He died on September 30, 1879, after being thrown from his buggy while visiting the Washington County Fair. He is buried at the Walker family cemetery on Mount Sequoyah.

Educational Stirrings

Fayetteville became known as the "Athens of the Ozarks" due its consistent support of advanced educational institutions and the general belief that education promoted better community and life. From the 1830s to the 1850s, four major educational institutions sprang to life, competing in Fayetteville for the best students, who came to Fayetteville from across Arkansas, Missouri and the Southwest.

The first efforts toward education in Fayetteville, though, occurred in the mid-1830s. In about 1835, a group of Fayetteville residents hired Robert W. Mecklin and Louisa Ann Mecklin as the first teachers of the Fayetteville Female Academy, the first chartered school in Fayetteville and only the second in the state. It was incorporated in 1836 but had been operating slightly before that year.

Robert Mecklin was a Methodist preacher, and he and his wife advertised that "the Bible shall be the standard of morals and religion" for their school.

The school continued in operation until 1843, when the Mecklins dissolved their connection to open the Ozark Institute at Mount Comfort. They operated the school in a building near the high point of what today is known as School Avenue and the site of Hillcrest Towers.[15]

Trail of Tears in 1839

Beginning with the presidency of Andrew Jackson, the American government began forcing members of the southern Indian nations out of their homelands and into the Indian Territory just west of Fayetteville. Members of the Cherokee Nation were forced out in the late 1830s, having contested the government's efforts through courts and public appeals for as long as they could. A group of relatively wealthy Cherokees, believing they could not avoid being forced out, signed the Treaty of New Echota in 1836, relinquishing their property in the East for land in the Indian Territory. The Treaty Party began moving west during 1837. The large majority of Cherokees who did not sign the treaty were forced out of their homes during 1838 and sent west, many of them finishing the journey in 1839. Three detachments of Cherokees came through parts of present-day Fayetteville.

The first detachment, one of the early Treaty Party groups led by B.B. Cannon, included approximately 360 Cherokees when it started west from the Cherokee Agency near Charleston, Tennessee. They followed what became known as the Northern Route, crossing Tennessee, Kentucky, southern Illinois and southern Missouri before coming into western Arkansas along the military road at Pea Ridge. The group faced severe weather during part of their trip that delayed their arrival by nearly a month compared to another detachment that had left at the same time but had stayed south and missed the bad weather. A number of ill and elderly Cherokees in the Cannon group died during the journey and were buried along the route. The surviving members arrived near Mount Comfort on December 25, 1837. The group "halted a half mile in advance of Mr. Cunningham's at a branch, 3 o'c P.M.," according to records kept by the Cannon group. Leaving Mount Comfort, they reached the Indian Territory on December 30. Significantly, this route Cannon followed proved to be the one that the largest portion of Cherokees used during the next year.[16]

However, the second detachment, led by John Benge, didn't follow that route. Instead, it left Alabama near the end of September 1838 and traveled overland to southwest Missouri, coming into Arkansas along the old Southwest Trail and then following the recently improved Arkansas Road across northern Arkansas. The members of the group arrived in Fayetteville on January 13, 1839, and camped along a creek and broad expanse of grassland near the present-day intersection of Martin Luther King Boulevard and Stadium Drive, where a small park and plaque commemorate their journey.

The Benge group numbered almost 1,200 people, including 114 enslaved people. The group was outfitted with sixty wagons and some six hundred horses. Over the course of the trip, thirty-three deaths and three births were recorded. One of the deaths occurred during a violent fight at Fayetteville. While stopped overnight in Fayetteville to restock and repair wagons, part of the Cherokee contingent went to the Fayetteville Square. Being Sunday, most of the saloons were closed except one, run by brothers Willis and Riley Wallace, who were described as having been involved in "numerous bloody affrays":

> *One Sabbath as the Indians were passing through to their homes from the east to the west, the Wallaces opened their grocery, which then meant whiskey shop. Soon many of the Indians were drunk and full of fight. The Wallaces not understanding their nature soon became engaged in the strife. A large half-blood, by the name of* [Nelson Orr], *attempted to stab* [Riley] *Wallace, when his brother Will rushed forward, and from behind the Indian and under his upraised arm, he plunged a large knife to his heart.*[17]

The Cherokee people were enraged by the murder and threatened to burn the town if Willis Wallace was not surrendered. Townspeople persuaded Wallace to flee town and then prevailed on the Cherokees to continue their journey with promises that Wallace would be tried in court. One writer of the time said that "Orr lingered several days in excruciating torture, and expired, as he had lived, a fearless desperado to the last."[18] Willis Wallace was tried in May, but he was acquitted of the murder charge.

In March 1839, another large group of Cherokees, led by Richard Taylor, followed the northern overland route and came into Arkansas along the Military Road from Springfield, Missouri, passing Pratt's store near the present-day Pea Ridge National Military Park and stopping for the night near Sugar Creek. During the night, the weather turned bad, with hail, wind and thunder. Rains prevented the group from moving during their second day in Arkansas. On the third day, the weather shifted to cloudy and cool, and the group traveled fifteen miles to Cross Hollows, where they ate dinner, and then another five miles to Fitzgerald's, on the northeast side of present-day Springdale, where they encamped. On the fourth day, Thursday, March 21, 1839, the Cherokees reached the Mount Comfort community on the northwest side of present-day Fayetteville and stayed near the Cunningham home. A doctor traveling with them split off to come into Fayetteville and described his short visit: "Fayetteville is in Washington County. Fertile land around it. Beautiful situation. A good Courthouse and bank house and saw other buildings. Had a mean meal at The Brick Tavern."[19]

From the Cunninghams', the Cherokees headed west on the fifth day to Cincinnati, probably traveling south through present-day Farmington. They then stayed near the home of Colonel Daniel and Mary Jane Thomason near Cincinnati. The next day, they arrived at Woodall in the Cherokee Nation. The Taylor group began with 1,029 members and arrived at the Indian Territory with 942; 55 members of the group died during the trip, and 15 children were born.[20]

Despite the Orr incident, the proximity of Fayetteville to the Cherokee Nation meant that a good deal of commerce occurred between the two regions, and prominent Cherokee families sent their children to Fayetteville for education.

ARRINGTON AND WALLACE WAR

The year 1839 proved to be a particularly violent year in the region surrounding Fayetteville. The killing of Nelson Orr as the Cherokees moved through town at the beginning of the year, the murder of a family in western Washington County and the assassinations of the Ridge family patriarchs on the border of the Indian Territory left people in the region deeply skeptical of the ability of lawful authorities to maintain peace and offer justice.

On the heels of this violence, Willis Wallace, recently acquitted of the stabbing murder of Orr, shot and killed another man, John Curry, for what one writer described as a "slight offence." Curry and three other men—L.D. Pollock, Thomas Wagnon and J. Wagnon—had come to Fayetteville and were playing a game of cards. Willis Wallace, Riley Wallace and a few other men resolved to stop the card playing, went to where the men were playing and threatened them with arrest. An altercation between the two factions occurred, and one of the Wagnons bolted, running across the Fayetteville Square and out the far side, with the Wallace group in pursuit:

> *Willis Wallace attempted to take Curry's horse from the rack, on the square, to pursue Wagnon. At this Curry pulled a pistol from his saddle-bags, but Wallace was too quick for him and, without waiting for further demonstrations, drew his own revolver and shot Curry dead. As he fired, Pollock, who was close by, threw a stone, striking Wallace upon the head and knocking him down, whereupon Riley Wallace, in a similar manner, struck down Pollock. He remained unconscious for several seconds. Meantime, Willis Wallace regained his feet, and going up to Pollock, plunged a bowie knife through his body, pinning him to the ground.*[21]

Amazingly, Pollock survived the stabbing because Dr. Thomas J. Pollard intervened, moved the injured man to a hotel and dressed his wounds.

The sheriff made several unsuccessful attempts to arrest Wallace, who had failed to appear for bond and was at large in the county. Attorney Alfred W. Arrington, incensed by Wallace's acquittal in the Orr case and lack of speedy trial in the Curry case, called a meeting southwest of Fayetteville near the Farmington Spring and asked the county's citizens to raise a force of between four hundred and five hundred volunteers to back the sheriff. They returned to Fayetteville and camped at Gallows Hill near the sheriff's forces.[22]

While Arrington was out of town, though, Wallace put out a call for friends and partisans, and they broke into the county's arsenal, acquiring two cannons and five hundred stand of arms. The Wallace faction fortified itself on the square using the Wallace grocery, a two-story storage building and a large warehouse. When the large Arrington group approached the square, it divided onto Mountain Street and Center Street, but each found a cannon pointed down the street at the members, halting them in their tracks. Meanwhile, the sheriff's group had approached from the east and gained control of the courthouse. Every window was filled with rifles and shotguns, pointed at the Wallace stronghold.

The next morning, Captain Mark Bean and eighty troopers of his light-horse brigade arrived from Cane Hill to aid Arrington and the sheriff, a move that disheartened the Wallace supporters. The next morning, Wallace's confederates began packing up to abandon their stronghold and return to their homes. A guard was sent to receive Willis Wallace, but he was told that Wallace was not there. A thorough search showed that he had indeed slipped out of town sometime during the night. Arrington called both sides to meet at McGarrah Grove, where he advised all to put away their guns and that the war was over.[23]

Wallace was eventually brought before a grand jury in the fall. His brother, Alfred Wallace, served as secretary of the jury, and Arrington claimed that Alfred Wallace failed to take down material parts of the testimony of witnesses. Willis Wallace was indicted for manslaughter but found guilty only of excusable homicide.[24]

Fayetteville Female Seminary

In 1823, a thirty-one-year-old woman named Sophia Sawyer left her home in New Hampshire and moved south to Tennessee as a missionary teacher of the American Board of Missions to the Cherokee Nation. She eventually landed among the Ridge and Boudinot families, tribal leaders in Georgia, and became an advocate for Cherokee children in general and girls specifically.

Financial support for the mission waned during the 1830s as it became clear that the United States would enforce removal of Native American nations from the eastern states. Nearly all the missionaries serving the Native American nations withdrew at least temporarily, but Sawyer remained with her charges.

John Ridge, the son of Cherokee chief Major Ridge, described Sawyer's situation:

> *She is a lady of fine feelings & susceptibilities of mind, and in the providence of God, unsupported and uncherished by any relations in this world....She enjoys our keenest sympathy, and ought to be supported by the approbation of the Board. If she is not, I can not answer for the pangs of heart affliction she will experience, when the ties which connect it with the Indians in her devoted labors shall be cut asunder.*[25]

When the Cherokees were forced west to the Indian Territory at the end of the decade, she came west as well. Not long after the Cherokees' arrival in the Indian Territory, the assassinations of the patriarchs of the Ridge and Boudinot families led those families and Sawyer to move to the safety of Fayetteville, where she and Sarah "Bird" Northrup Ridge opened the Fayetteville Female

Seminary in 1839 in a log building on the Fayetteville Square. It was soon moved to the upstairs of a storefront, the lower half inhabited by the town's "thespian society," sinful actors whom the students were ordered to avoid on their way to and from school. By mid-1840, she had fifty-one students, and Judge David Walker and his wife, Jane, then deeded part of their land to the school consisting of several acres of property along the south side of Mountain Street running the full block between Locust and School Avenues, overlooking "a beautiful valley, mountains and woodland in the distance."[26]

Fayetteville's first newspaper, the *Witness*, published by C.F. Town, advertised that a "new and convenient edifice has been erected for the use of the school. This is located in a retired part of town; and, offers every facility to the young ladies to take exercise without exposure." Tuition for a five-month session ran eight dollars for basic classes and ten dollars for more advance branches of study. Boarding could be had with the "most respectable families" for two dollars per week.[27]

From the beginning, the seminary was open to young women of both European American ancestry and Native American descent, primarily Cherokee families who already knew of Sawyer's reputation as a teacher. She and her Cherokee students lived at the home of James H. and Catherine Stirman.

Throughout the first half of the 1840s, her enrollment grew and the campus expanded to include boarding space, more often provided by Fayetteville families. She advertised in the state's newspapers and the *Cherokee Advocate*, published at Tahlequah. The larger student body allowed Sawyer to coax noted educators such as Robert Mecklin and Cephas Washburn to teach at the school.

Sawyer modeled her school after that of her own schoolmate, Mary Lyon, who had founded Mount Holyoke School in Massachusetts two years earlier. In the Fayetteville Female Seminary's primary department, the school taught reading, spelling, penmanship, arithmetic, geography, grammar and the history of the United States. The four-year general curriculum included courses in algebra, zoology, astronomy, botany, philosophy, chemistry, geology, geometry and natural theology. Music, both vocal and instrumental, was taught throughout the four years.

One researcher described the regimen of Sawyer and her seminary:

> *She held every girl to strict account. On Sunday mornings the girls walked in dignified lines, two and two, to church, with Miss Sawyer at the head and her assistant, Miss Foster, at the rear. At six each morning, Miss*

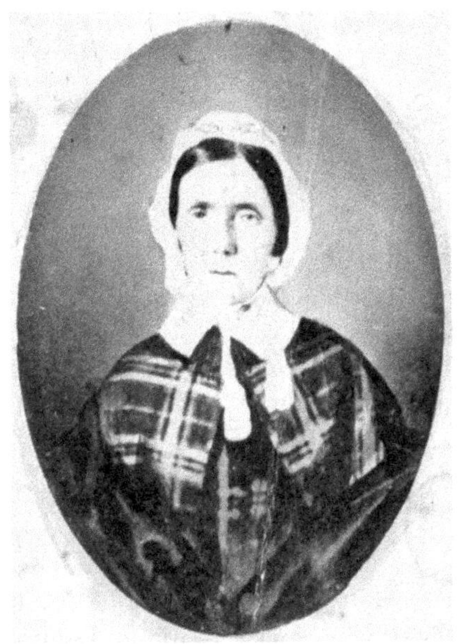

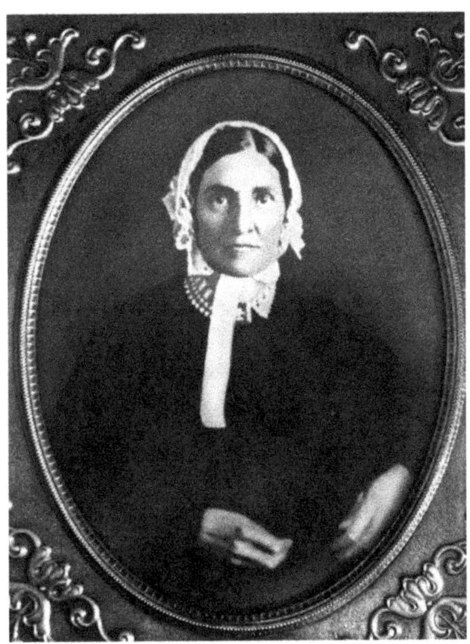

Left: Sophia Sawyer, co-founder of the Fayetteville Female Seminary. *Courtesy Special Collections, University of Arkansas Libraries.*

Right: Sarah Bird Northrup Ridge, co-founder of the Fayetteville Female Seminary. *Courtesy Washington County Historical Society.*

> *Sawyer opened the stair door and called, "Spring, young ladies!" They were required to walk a mile before breakfast in order to make their cheeks rosy and to give them an appetite for the morning meal, which consisted of hot cakes, butter, weak syrup, and weaker tea. Young ladies were expected to be dainty in their eating. At night, after study hour, the tinkle of a little silver bell called the girls to the study hall for prayer. After vespers, the girls went to their respective rooms and to bed.*[28]

The school ran into a rough patch between 1846 and 1848 after Sawyer hired a teacher named Ann James. Sawyer and James did not see eye to eye, and James was also ill for a period and unable to fulfill her teaching duties. Sawyer brought in brother and sister Harmaun and Harmania Freyschlag to teach the fine arts courses. James eventually left the school, working with Robert Mecklin to develop a competing female seminary near Mount Comfort, a complement to his male Ozark Institute.

To replace James, Sawyer soon hired a recent graduate of Mount Holyoke, Lucretia Foster, who settled into Fayetteville. In the early 1850s,

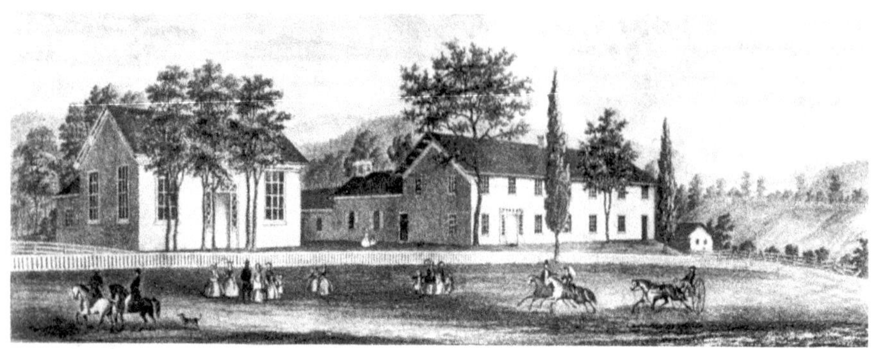

The Fayetteville Female Seminary, established in 1839, was designed after the New England boarding schools in which co-founder Sophia Sawyer was educated. *Courtesy Washington County Historical Society.*

Sawyer hired two more faculty members: Mary Daniels, another Mount Holyoke graduate, and Ferdinand F. Zellner, who taught music and wrote several popular tunes, including "The Fayetteville Polka," that are the first-known compositions by an Arkansan to be published.

By this time, the school enrollment totaled between 100 and 150 students each year, an impressive size for a town of only 600 people. The campus comprised the entire city block and included four buildings of New England design facing Mountain Street. One student wrote of this period:

> *On my arrival at Miss Sawyer's Female Seminary I didn't understand the situation of things. I observed that whenever Miss Sawyer made her appearance every girl present began to dodge out of sight, and find a place of retreat....Miss Sawyer was a first-class regulator and my position with the old lady was either up in the zenith or down in the depths. As a rule I could please her, but occasionally, like all the others, I woefully missed it, and in a short time I learned to take my part in getting out of sight when the commanding officer hove into view.*[29]

Sawyer died of tuberculosis in 1854 and was initially buried on the grounds of the school. She willed the school to the American Board of Commissioners of Foreign Missions, which in turn sold the school to Mary Daniels, who by that time had married Presley Smith. She partnered with Lucretia Foster, who had married Presley's son, Jack Smith. Lucretia Foster Smith became principal and led the school during the next seven to eight years, until the Civil War forced its closing. In 1859, the school enrolled 103 students. The school continued in operation at a much lower capacity when the Civil War began. In 1862, Zellner purchased a share in the school. After serving as a hospital after the Battle of Prairie Grove, the major building of the campus caught fire and was destroyed. Foster died in 1863, and Zellner moved to California. After the war, Sawyer's body was reinterred at the new public cemetery, Evergreen, a marble obelisk erected by her students marking her grave.

Far West Seminary and Ozark Institute

In 1843, likely spurred by the success of Sophia Sawyer's female seminary, several leaders in the region began agitating and planning for a collegiate-level institution. The state had failed to use its federal grant to create a state university, so Cephas Washburn, who had founded Dwight Mission, the first Cherokee school in the Arkansas Territory, led the group. They gathered at the Mount Comfort Meetinghouse about five miles northwest of the Fayetteville Square.

They decided on a name for the school, the Far West Seminary, to emphasize its frontier location. Solomon Tuttle donated a piece of land that included a spring near where present-day Deane Solomon Road crosses Clabber Creek.

Aside from Washburn, several leading residents joined the effort, including Alfred Arrington, Isaac Murphy and David Walker. They proposed a constitution for the school, including a philosophy that the school should never "possess a sectarian character in religion or a party character in politics."

A board of visitors with membership including U.S. Representative John Smith Phelps and judge Charles S. Yancey, both of Springfield, Missouri; Jesse Busheyhead of the Cherokee Nation; and George Washington Paschal of Van Buren demonstrated the desire of the organizers to recruit students from across a similarly wide region on the American frontier.

Democratic opposition to the school arose in the Arkansas legislature because many of its proponents were Whigs. The Democrats nearly prevented the school from receiving a charter, prompting the editor of the *Arkansas Gazette* to assert that for Democrats it is "a principle with them never to encourage institutions of learning." Nevertheless, the legislature did approve a charter, and subscriptions provided funding to build the school.

The organizers contracted with William D. Cunningham to build a brick school building. Unfortunately, a fire gutted the building on February 27, 1845, just before the school was to open.

Historian Michael Dougan wrote, "Far West Seminary is arguably the most important school that Arkansas never had, given that those involved with it later participated in other educational ventures."[30]

One of those who did so was Robert Mecklin, another member of the Far West Seminary's board of visitors. He had already begun planning a primary school to complement the higher education of the Far West Seminary. Despite its loss, he continued forward, building the Ozark Institute in 1845 near the abandoned Far West campus, looking out over the broad prairie and farmland surrounding Clabber Creek. The main building was two stories high and comprised more than 3,200 square feet of space. A wide hall the length of the building separated four rooms.

Families from across Northwest Arkansas and the Indian Territory sent their sons to the institute, and within four years, the Ozark Institute had a student body of sixty boys. Among its students were John Rollin Ridge, the first Native American known to have published a novel; James H. Van Hoose, later a mayor of Fayetteville; Edward Payson Washburn, the painter of *The Arkansas Traveler*; and John Lynch Adair, later the editor of the *Cherokee Advocate*.

In 1848, tuition for the year was $24.00, according to a notice published in the *Arkansas State Democrat*, and room and board could be found with "respectable" families near the school for $1.25 per week. By the mid-1850s, tuition varied from $8.00 to $15.00 per term depending on the class entered.

In addition to Mecklin, other teachers included A.S. Lockert, Peter Van Hoose, Cephas Washburn, Isaac Murphy, David McMannus and Robert Graham, who eventually left the school in the early 1850s to start Arkansas College.

The school continued until the Civil War, when Confederate troops took over the campus for an encampment, using the main building for a hospital. Among the earliest casualties of the war were William Brown and Henry Fulbright, former students of the institute who died at the Battle of Wilson's Creek, the first battle of the Trans-Mississippi theater.

The school building survived the war, and the institute reopened in 1868 under the leadership of principal Charles H. Leverett. Mecklin died in 1871, and Leverett left the school in 1872 to teach at the newly established Arkansas Industrial University.

Today, a few stones and a marker next to the clubhouse of the defunct Razorback Golf Course designate the site of the school.

Arkansas College

Although the lure of the California Gold Rush of 1849 coaxed some Fayetteville residents into abandoning their families and homes temporarily to go west in search of fortune, those who stayed behind suffered neither the pains of the desert nor the pangs of disappointment that most 49ers found in the gold fields. Most returned home as soon as a steamer to the Isthmus of Panama could be arranged, and few stayed more than a year. By 1850, there were six dry goods stores and two groceries in Fayetteville. "People from King's River and War Eagle country, from Benton and Crawford Counties and the Indian Nation, bought all their goods here."[31]

The founding of Arkansas College benefited from this commerce of people, and in turn, the community benefited from the college.

When George Washington Grayson rode slowly into Fayetteville in 1859 for the first time, the town was growing economically and culturally. It boasted two hotels, perhaps a dozen mercantiles, a steam-powered mill, a newspaper and nearly one thousand residents. Grayson had come to attend Arkansas College and was one of three students for whom the Creek Nation had provided tuition. He was only sixteen, and his parents had misgivings about sending him so far away but relented because of his desire to continue the successful learning that he had already acquired at Asbury Mission school.

His three- to four-day horse ride from a log cabin at North Fork Town, just west of present-day Eufaula, Oklahoma, to the up-and-coming town of Fayetteville was also a journey into a new world for Grayson, just as it was

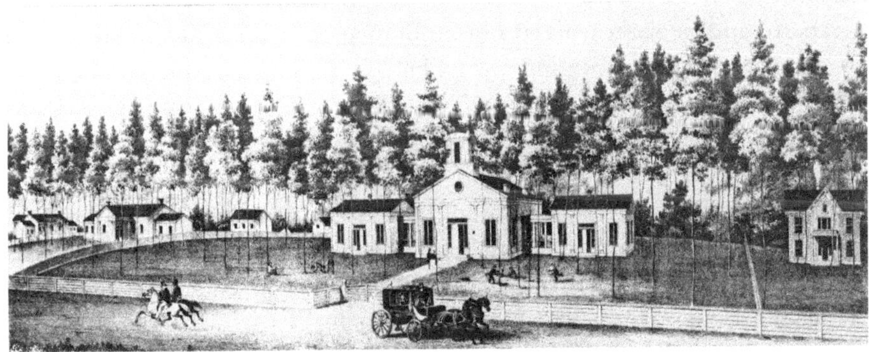

The campus of Arkansas College in the mid- to late 1850s included the main academic building, a library to the right and the home of the college president to the left. The building at far left, the Tebbetts House, is still standing and used by the Washington County Historical Society as its headquarters. *Courtesy Washington County Historical Society.*

for most of the college's students: "Everything was entirely different, and in most respects superior to anything I had ever seen or was accustomed to in the simple life I had hitherto led at my humble cabin homes in the forest of the Creek Nation, or the school at Asbury."[32]

Arkansas College, known as the Fayetteville Male Academy for its first two years, was eight years old by the time Grayson arrived. It was founded in late 1850 by Reverend Robert Graham. Graham was from Liverpool, England, but immigrated to America in his youth, apprenticing as a carpenter in Allegheny, Pennsylvania, and then moving to Bethany, Virginia, to help build Bethany College, a school supported by founders of the Christian Church, Disciples of Christ. He became a student at Bethany, and upon graduation, he accepted a mission from the college to travel among the Disciple followers living in the Southwest, spending a significant amount of time in Arkansas and reporting the status of the followers back to the college.

Arriving in Fayetteville in 1848, Graham and his wife, Mariah, helped establish the Christian Church, and he became the congregation's first pastor, also teaching at the Ozark Institute to supplement his income. One biography described him as having a "bright, florid complexion" and large light-blue eyes: "He is a ready extemporaneous speaker, and, on a great occasion, is capable of exercising wonderful power over an audience. He possesses a strong, active, sympathetic nature, and this gives him great influence in the social circle. Few men have more ability to control the masses."[33]

He left the Ozark Institute to found a male academy of higher education, which initially met in a home at the corner of present-day Dickson Street and St. Charles Avenue. Two blocks away, though, a piece of property tempted Graham, and he soon worked out an agreement with William McGarrah to purchase ten acres fronting a road known then as the Missouri Road. It spanned a block between present-day Dickson and Spring Streets. Soon, as a result of Graham's college, Missouri Road would become better known as College Avenue.

Nathaniel Ragland, a later pastor of the Christian Church, quoted Graham as saying, "The erection of the main building was begun immediately. It was large and elegant. Later two wings and a library room were added, making it one of the most complete colleges in the state."[34]

The Arkansas General Assembly on December 14, 1852, approved an act to allow the college "to confer the degree of Doctor…and other academical degrees," the first degree-conferring institution chartered by the state. The next day, the legislature chartered the earlier-established Cane Hill College in southwest Washington County. Arkansas College awarded its first seven bachelor's degrees in 1854.

From its beginning, Arkansas College attracted students from across the frontier portions of Arkansas, Missouri, Texas and the Indian Territory, as well as several students as far away as England. At its height, the college enrolled about two hundred students per year. By 1859, tuition was $225 for the normal September–June term. Students boarded at homes in Fayetteville, and George W. Grayson recalled lodging at the residence of Joe Lewis "up in town" along with several other college boys.

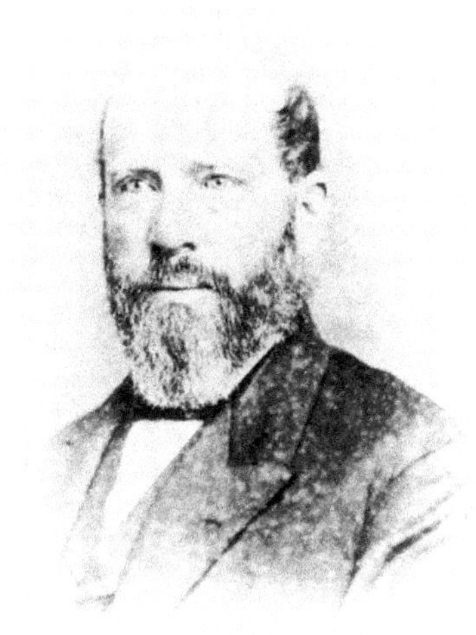

Robert Graham, the founder of Arkansas College. *Courtesy First Christian Church.*

Grayson quickly became friends with the other two Creek students, William McIntosh and Eli Jacobs, and the only Cherokee student at the time, Saladin Watie. They all probably felt the initial loneliness and separateness that Grayson recalled:

> *I was completely struck with awe and wonderment at my new surroundings. Here was a school where the pupils spoke not a word of Indian; scarcely a boy to be seen with jet black eyes and hair as were my late schoolmates at Asbury; their sports different; their apparel* [was] *also different in material and make from mine. As I could clearly see, my uncouth appearance drew many eyes toward me to my sheer embarrassment. It was clear too that I was being regarded very much as* [are]*...children at the side shows of a circus, the ugly specimen of humanity said by the obliging manager to be the only living "Wild man of Borneo."*[35]

Grayson successfully stayed throughout the year, forming immediate friendships with the three other Native Americans and eventual friendships with the European American students. He also took to the aesthetics of his Anglo schoolmates: "Time passed on, however, and I became more civilized and more careful of my apparel and personal appearance, and thereafter had my clothing cut and sewed by the city tailor, and in the prevailing style."

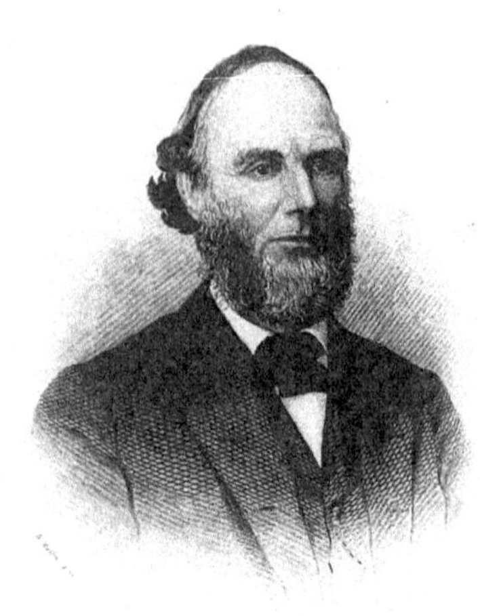

William Baxter, president of Arkansas College at the time of the Civil War. *Author's collection.*

Like many of Arkansas College's graduates, Grayson went on to be a leader in his own community and for the Creek Nation, in general, serving in a variety of roles, including as principal chief from 1917 until his death in 1920.

In 1859, Graham joined the faculty of Kentucky University at Harrodsburg, Kentucky. In his place was hired William Baxter, "small of stature, but compactly built." He was born in Leeds, England, and his family immigrated to America in 1828. Baxter was a graduate of Bethany College and a professor at Newton College in Woodville, Mississippi, when he was hired as the second president of Arkansas College.

After a year in Kentucky, Graham returned to Fayetteville, aiding Baxter in teaching but also focusing on development of the college's financial support in the state. Their efforts were cut short during the spring of 1861, when Arkansas voted to secede from the Union. Baxter described his efforts to hold the college together:

> *Up to the month of March, 1861, the studies had suffered but little interruption; at the close of the first term in January, and on the 22d of February, several addresses were made, mostly in a loyal tone, and some of them in a spirit warmly patriotic; only one or two inclining to the Southern view of affairs....Knowing that the storm could not be averted, I strove in some degree to guide it, and therefore, while admitted the right of both sides to speak their sentiments, I urged the propriety of regarding each other's convictions, for both might be sincere.*[36]

Students from Arkansas College began withdrawing in the spring before the end of the school year to join companies, and the school closed its doors for what Baxter and Graham hoped would be a short period. Fayetteville became a forward post for the Confederate army. The college campus soon became campgrounds for troops out of Louisiana through the remainder of 1861.

The Confederate troops withdrew from the city in late February 1862 due to advancing Union troops. Confederates burned many of the buildings that had been used for storage of military supplies or were deemed to have strategic military importance. The main college survived this initial conflagration, but it was destroyed on March 4, 1862, by Confederate troops as they headed back north through Fayetteville on their way to the Battle of Pea Ridge. Pro-Union sentiments of the college founders and many of the church members may have contributed to the decision by the Confederates to burn the campus.

Graham and Baxter fled the city at different times to reach safety in the North. Graham briefly went to California, where organizers of the Pacific College in Santa Rosa had offered him a position. He returned to Kentucky University at Harrodsburg, where he taught until 1896. Baxter and his family wound up settling in Cincinnati, Ohio. As with the Fayetteville Female Seminary, the pride that Fayettevillians felt for Arkansas College led to Fayetteville's successful bid for the state's first public university after the war.

Butterfield Overland Mail

By the mid-1850s, commerce between the eastern United States and California caused Congress to seek faster ways to transmit mail, which up to that time had usually been sent by ship to the Isthmus of Panama and transferred overland to more ships waiting on the Pacific side to take it north to San Francisco. The amount of time involved amounted to two or three months.

On March 3, 1857, Congress authorized U.S. Postmaster General Aaron Brown to contract for transportation of the U.S. mail overland from the Mississippi River to the West Coast. Rather than follow the well-established northern overland route used by migrants and freight wagons, John Butterfield and his associates proposed a route with eastern starting points in St. Louis, Missouri, and Memphis, Tennessee, that would join at Fort Smith and then cross the desert southwest, where snow would be a rare occurrence. The route was criticized for the scarcity of water and stock through the region, and the 2,800-mile route was perceived to be too long to be covered in the twenty-five days specified by Congress. Nevertheless, the ability to provide year-round service persuaded Aaron Brown to award a six-year contract for an Overland Mail Company to Butterfield at the rate of $600,000 per year.

Initially, Brown specified that the mails from St. Louis and Memphis should merge at Little Rock, Arkansas, and proceed to Preston, Texas, and then west to San Francisco. In terms of speed, examination of the routes showed that Fort Smith would be a better juncture point for the two eastern legs, and Postmaster Brown acquiesced on the matter, which meant that the route from St. Louis would come through Fayetteville.

Out of St. Louis, Butterfield chose a route that allowed him to use the Pacific Railroad as far as its westernmost rail terminus at Tipton, Missouri. There the mails were to be switched to stagecoach and headed south along the Boonville Road through Springfield, Missouri, and then onward along the Military Road into Fayetteville. From Fayetteville, the path led over the rugged Boston Mountain Road to Van Buren.

Butterfield established major stables at Fayetteville on the present-day site of the Historic Washington County Courthouse. The company quartered four stagecoaches and eighteen horses in the town.[37] Butterfield also put his son, Charles Butterfield, in charge of the operations at Fayetteville, which included creating a hotel for passengers who wanted a break from the constant rattle of stagecoaches.

The westbound route through Fayetteville came in from the north across the eastern side of present-day Lake Fayetteville Park. The city has preserved part of the trail, which is now in the National Register of Historic Places, and erected an interpretive sign about the Butterfield route. The stagecoaches then followed along the present-day roads of Old Missouri Road, Old Wire Road and Mission Boulevard, which at that time angled over to join Dickson Street. Then the stagecoaches followed present-day College Avenue to Center Street and onto the square.

Margaret Blakemore Taylor described the arrival of the Butterfield coach from the north. The conductor of the coach would blow a horn near the Gunter place, and the help at Byrnside's Tavern on the square would "put the meal on the table, and the stable boys would have fresh horses ready for the coach" by the time it arrived on the square.[38]

Waterman Ormsby, a reporter for the *New York Herald*, rode the first stage west and described his own entry to Fayetteville:

> *The route leads over those steep and rugged hills which surround the Ozark range in this section of Arkansas, and we were just three hours going from Callahan's to Fayetteville. This town is located up among the hills, in a*

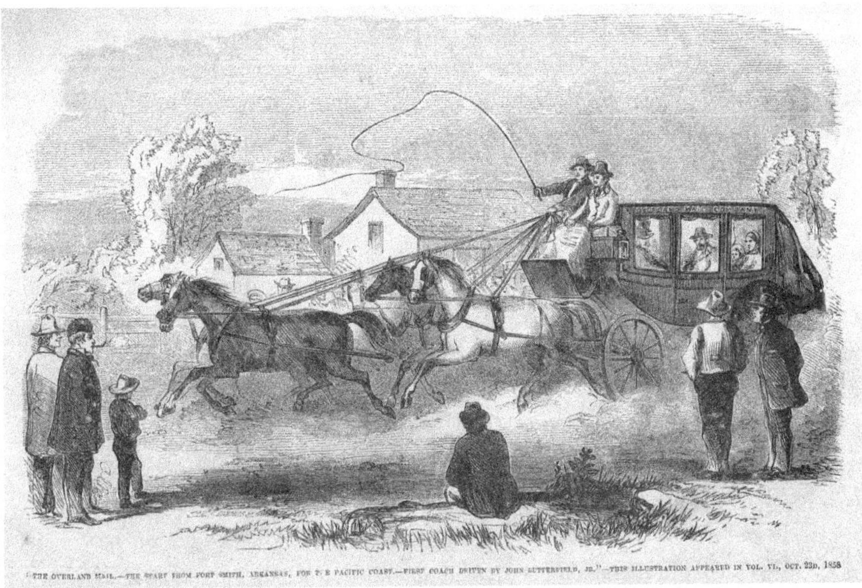

An 1858 lithograph from *Harper's Magazine* depicts the first run of the Butterfield Overland Mail Company's transcontinental stage operation. *Author's collection.*

> *most inaccessible spot…said by its inhabitants to be the star county of the state. It has two churches, the county court house, a number of fine stores and dwellings, and, I believe, about 1,800 inhabitants. It is a flourishing little town, and its deficiency of a good hotel will, I understand, be supplied by Mr. Butterfield, who has bought some property for that purpose.*

Another stage passenger described Fayetteville as "a go-ahead place possessing its pillared court-house, churches, and ladies' college."[39]

Leaving out of town, the route went east on Mountain Street past the Fayetteville Female Seminary and meandered through the roads of southwest Fayetteville before hitting Cato Springs Road and heading for Hogeye. Its path between Fayetteville and Fort Smith went over the Boston Mountain range of the Ozarks, and horses were traded for mules along this broken stretch, usually at Parks' Station southwest of Fayetteville:

> *I had thought before we reached this point that the roads of Missouri and Arkansas could not be equalled; but here Arkansas fairly beats itself.*
>
> *I might say our road was steep, rugged, jagged, rough, and mountainous—and then wish for some more expressive words in the*

> *language. Had not Mr. Crocker provided a most extraordinary team I doubt whether we should have been able to cross in less than two days. The wiry, light, little animals tugged and pulled as if they would tear themselves to pieces, and our heavy wagon bounded along the crags as if it would be shaken in pieces every minute, and ourselves disembowelled* [sic] *on the spot.*[40]

William Tallack, an Englishman returning home after a visit to Australia, came west on the Butterfield stage and reported having to get out of the stage and walk part of the route over the Boston Mountains because of the steep grade. He wrote:

> *Last night we crossed Boston Mountain, a spur of the Ozarks. Hour after hour we clambered literally 'upstairs,' for our route lay at times in the channel of a mountain stream, over successive ledges of rock. The worst of the ascent we had to walk, which was more comfortable than when inside, as there was bright moonlight. The scenery of the deep gorge was very romantic, and fireflies were swarming around us in every direction.*[41]

At first glance, the speedy passing of stagecoaches through Fayetteville would seem to add little more commerce than the romantic fireflies. The Butterfield Overland Mail, however, boosted Fayetteville's finances in ways both direct and indirect. Aside from the passengers who stopped briefly for food at Byrnside's or spent a night at the Butterfield Hotel, the operation had a much deeper effect as a catalyst for other commercial opportunities. Manufacturing operations such as wagon-building shops, blacksmiths and tanneries, the increased ease of travel for students coming to the Fayetteville Female Seminary or Arkansas College and a growth in the number of merchants competing in Fayetteville were all a direct effect of the Butterfield route.

The improved route also became known as one assured path through the western frontier to Texas, so many of the immigrants heading west followed the route through Fayetteville. One early county resident, Samuel Marrs, wrote to a friend about how the "overland mail has caused a heap of people to look along the line for homes. There is a heap of travel done in the stages as they are regular."[42]

Fayetteville Female Institute

In 1858, the state General Assembly passed an act to incorporate the Fayetteville Female Institute under patronage of the Baptist denomination. The school began classes in early 1859, with Thomas B. Van Horne in charge. The Baptist Convention raised $41,000 for an endowment in 1859 that had risen to $75,000 by October 1860.

The school came into direct competition with the Fayetteville Female Seminary (and was in some measure intended to do so). Some families in Fayetteville did not want their daughters attending school with the Cherokees or taking classes under German teachers such as Ferdinand Zellner or the Freyschlag family.

The school offered a similar curriculum of reading, arithmetic, vocal music, grammar, composition, geography, algebra, geometry, trigonometry, physiology, botany, geology, zoology, chemistry, philosophy, astronomy, natural theology and "evidences of Christianity."[43]

Uniforms were required for students, who wore a costume of pink calico or lawn dresses with white aprons and bonnets in the summer and maroon woolen dresses with green hoods, red silk lining and dark aprons for common use during the winter. Although under Baptist sponsorship, the school allowed students to attend such places of worship as their parents designated.

On January 7, 1861, the school was reincorporated with a new name, the Northwestern Arkansas Baptist Female Institute. Van Horne still headed the school, but its service was cut short when the Civil War interrupted all educational institutions in Fayetteville. The building was chosen as an arsenal and cartridge manufactory for the Confederate troops who made Fayetteville their base of operations at the beginning of the war.

The school building and all buildings deemed to have military importance were set on fire by Confederate forces fleeing Fayetteville at the approach of Union troops.

A Decade of Economic Growth

The 1850s proved to be one of Fayetteville's largest growth periods. Along with the establishment of Arkansas College, the town saw the construction of the state's first steam-powered mill, reestablishment of a newspaper and an influx of merchants, tradespeople and skilled professionals, many coming from northern states. Elias C. Boudinot was among the arrivals. Like his cousins, the Ridges, he came west during the forced Cherokee removal, and his father was killed soon after arrival by a rival faction of Cherokees. Boudinot drew inspiration from his older cousin, John Rollin Ridge, and became a writer. He recalled his first trip to Fayetteville in 1854:

> *Never shall I forget my impressions of the town as I halted my poney on the hights* [sic] *near A.M. Wilson's house and looked at the lights shining from many a dwelling. Aeneas Ridge was the only person I knew in that strange town, and yet I felt that I was near home and friends; it was very dark and raining, and I called at the gate of Maj. Reagan's house for instructions, a servant piloted me to the residence of Mrs. Ridge who lived in the one story house opposite the present residence of S.K. Stone, but at that time the home of Judge David Walker of the Supreme Court. I was most cordially received; and after a few happy days I turned my face school-ward* [to the Indian Territory] *with regrets, but with a determination to return in the Spring and read law in the office of Col. A.M. Wilson.*[44]

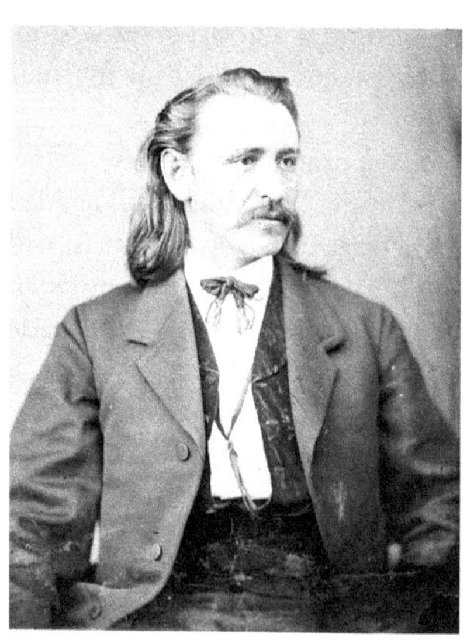

Elias C. Boudinot, a Cherokee lawyer and newspaper publisher who lived in Fayetteville during the 1850s, pictured here sometime between 1860 and 1875. *Courtesy Library of Congress Prints and Photographs Division, Brady-Handy Photograph Collection.*

Boudinot did, in fact, return the next year, reading law under Wilson and becoming acquainted with the leading residents of Fayetteville. In 1858, he and another lawyer, J.R. Pettigrew, began publishing the *Arkansian*, a newspaper that soon drew readership across Northwest Arkansas and the Indian Territory. A competing newspaper, the *Fayetteville Democrat*, began publishing in 1860. That same year, on July 4, the Stebbins telegraph connected Fayetteville with St. Louis, the first telegraph to reach Arkansas. Pettigrew sent a message to the mayor of St. Louis, who replied in kind. Suddenly, the news from across America was available at the Fayetteville Square within a day of its occurrence. No longer did a newspaper have to wait a month to report the inauguration of a president. And the great newspapers on America's eastern seaboard began running stories datelined from Fayetteville, including the latest news being brought from California by the Butterfield stage and the occasional note about Fayetteville itself, such as the weather report in the *New York Times* that snow had "commenced falling about noon and is still falling."[45] The growth and productivity bode well for the town.

James H. Van Hoose, who arrived in Fayetteville in 1852, wrote later of that decade, "These school girls and the young men of Arkansas College, together with the young men of the town and our own beautiful girls made Fayetteville society second to none in the state: in fact from 1851 to 1861 there were very few towns in the South or West the size of ours where there could be found more prosperous business men, more gallant beaux, more charming and beautiful young ladies, better schools or a more intelligent, industrious, happy and contented people than our own loved Fayetteville could produce."[46]

CHAPTER 3

THE CIVIL WAR

The election of Abraham Lincoln as president proved a catalyst for seven Southern states to secede from the United States during December 1860 and January 1861, even before his inauguration. Reaction in Northwest Arkansas was milder, but two statewide ballot issues were put to voters, the first regarding whether the state should secede and the second to approve a convention to consider secession and elect delegates to it. The voters, of course, were all white men. Neither women nor African Americans had yet been given the right to vote.

Generally, residents in the mountainous northern and western parts of the state were in favor of maintaining the Union, and those living in the southern and eastern parts of the state, where agricultural enterprises relied heavily on slave labor, were in favor of secession.

Fayetteville leaned toward maintaining the Union, although secession sentiments ran high, too. Even among the Unionists, however, very little support could be detected for abolition. The *Arkansian* newspaper, for instance, was established in 1858 with one of its missions being "to stay the onrushing tide of abolitionism, which threatens to overwhelm the South."[47] In another instance, a city committee held hearings to consider the case of a man named E. White, "who has expressed sentiments so unfriendly to the South as to provoke threats of forcible expulsion if he continued longer in the community." In deciding how to deal with White, the chair of the committee resigned his post in order to write a minority opinion. James R. Pettigrew, a lawyer and former editor of the *Arkansian*, was selected to present the majority report, which essentially told White to get out of town.[48]

In the run-up to the election, sentiments ran high on both sides of the question. On February 2, two weeks before the election, between four hundred and five hundred men met in Fayetteville to consider resolutions that had been adopted by a convention at nearby Boonsboro and to put forward a slate of delegates to represent the region at the Secession Convention. After the reading of these resolutions, Dr. G.W. Taylor moved that a committee of fifteen be appointed to draft a report expressive of the sense of the meeting, whereupon Fayetteville mayor Stephen Bedford took the floor and charged that the chairman for this committee had been selected a week before, that the resolutions to be reported by the committee were already prepared and that the secretaries—James H. Van Hoose and M.C. Duke—were secessionists. These charges threw the meeting into turmoil. The *Arkansian* newspaper reported that "the noise and uproar [were] almost deafening; the Judge's stand, the Clerk's desk, railing and every other commanding position was occupied by excited individuals using harsh and violent language, weapons freely handled, pistols cocked and knives loosened in their scabbards." The meeting was then abruptly adjourned *sine die* and without nomination of delegates to the state convention.[49]

Instead, delegates were elected at large. Arkansas voters turned down secession when they voted on February 18. Washington County voters were strongly against secession, voting 1,541 to 569 against it. However, voters statewide approved the proposal to hold a convention to consider secession. Fayetteville voters approved a pro-Union slate of delegates, as did most of the counties in the northern and western parts of the state.

While President Lincoln was being inaugurated on March 4 in Washington, D.C., the convention to consider secession opened at the statehouse in Little Rock. Delegates elected attorney David Walker of Fayetteville as president of the convention and attorney Elias C. Boudinot, who had recently moved from Fayetteville to Little Rock, as secretary.

Meanwhile, in Fayetteville, a meeting was held at the Washington County Courthouse and chaired by Judge Benjamin J.H. Gaines "to take the sense of the people on the inauguration of A. Lincoln." Most of the members were associated with the secessionist elements of Fayetteville, and a resolution was passed calling for the state to take steps "as would guarantee her safety"; however, reports indicated that Union sentiments continued to prevail.

Back in Little Rock, the Unionist delegates carried the day at the state convention, defeating the secession proposal, thirty-nine to thirty-five, on March 16, but the Unionist delegates eventually agreed to allow the matter of secession to be put again to a popular vote in early August. The Unionists also tacitly agreed that should the federal government coerce seceded states to rejoin the Union, the dynamic might swing sentiment in favor of secession.

Far from calming matters, though, the delegates' decision catalyzed partisans on both sides. The *New York Times* reported that "an immense crowd assembled [in Fayetteville], which was addressed by Secessionists and Unionists" on April 8. The "States Rights Party" in Fayetteville raised a large flag containing red and white stripes, mottoes and fifteen stars, one for each slave state. Supporters of the Union flew a federal flag from the courthouse with thirty-four stars, one for each state, including those that had voted to secede.[50]

On April 12, South Carolina troops bombarded Fort Sumter after Federal troops refused to surrender the fort. Lincoln called on the states, including Arkansas, to supply volunteers to put down the insurgency, but Arkansas governor Henry Massie Rector refused. One week later, President Lincoln ordered a blockade of Southern ports, limiting the ability of the Confederate States of America to import needed goods for war.

David Walker reconvened the state delegates to the Secession Convention, and the delegates voted for Arkansas to secede from the United States. Five members voted against secession, but Walker asked that a second vote be cast and that the five dissenters change their votes to show unanimity for secession. Isaac Murphy, a former Fayetteville resident serving as a delegate from Madison County, remained unmoved by talk of unanimity regarding the question of disunion and was the only delegate to vote against secession on the second ballot. On May 18, Arkansas was admitted to the Confederate States of America.

During May and June, military companies began forming across the state. At Fayetteville, the Pike Guards were organized and assigned as Company C to Colonel John R. Gratiot's Arkansas State Troops. Americus Rieff organized Rieff's Mounted Company of the Arkansas State Troops. The company served as an independent cavalry troop, reporting directly to Confederate general Benjamin McCulloch.

Troops from Louisiana and Texas began converging on Fayetteville, which became the central point of Confederate strength west of the Mississippi River. The campuses of Arkansas College and the Ozark Institute became encampments for the military units. The county courthouse at the center of the Fayetteville Square became a headquarters for McCulloch.

By the end of June, the city was on a war footing, with a mix of fearless bravado for the war ahead but also a certain realization that much was already lost. One resident made it clear:

> *All at once we awoke to the fact that we were in the Confederacy, within the Southern lines. The mails stopped, newspapers ceased to be seen, men began to look at the resources of the country, and soon the fact stared every man in the face, that for nearly every necessity, and all the luxuries of life, we had hitherto been dependent on the now hated North. Hardware, school-books, stationery, dry-goods, medicines, implements of agriculture, groceries, carpets, hats, shoes, pins, needles, matches, almanacs, nay every thing, one might say, were now foreign articles.*[51]

War Begins in the Trans-Mississippi

Confederate troops under General Benjamin McCulloch moved north in late July 1861, leaving their stronghold at Fayetteville to join the Missouri State Guard in southwest Missouri. Their intent was to push Federal troops back to St. Louis and bring Missouri in league with the secessionist states. Union troops under Brigadier General Nathaniel Lyon were encamped at Springfield, Missouri. Although both leaders were planning attacks, Lyon got the jump, attacking the Confederate forces at first light on August 10.

They were camped along the valley of Wilson's Creek and its surrounding hillsides, about one hundred miles northeast of Fayetteville. Lyon's troops pushed through the first Rebel camps and took high ground that became known as "Bloody Hill."

Confederate troops charged Union lines three times but were unable to break them. General Lyon, however, was shot dead in the heart after being wounded twice. The Union troops withdrew to Springfield initially and then to Rolla, Missouri, giving the Confederates a victory that became known as the "Bull Run of the West." Without sufficient organization, ammunition or a supply line, though, General McCulloch ordered the Confederate forces back to Arkansas, a decision that disheartened Confederate sympathizers in Missouri.

About 2,500 soldiers died during the battle, including the first Fayetteville casualties. The bodies of Captain S.R. Bell, Sergeant Williman Brown and Privates Samuel McCurdy and Henry Fulbright were returned from

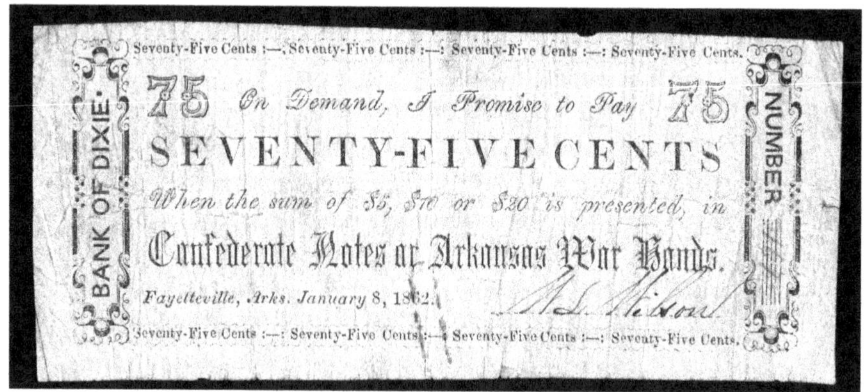

After Union money was withdrawn and before Confederate currency made its way into Arkansas circulation, a Bank of Dixie sprang up in Fayetteville in early 1862. It issued scrip, as did several businesses, such as Stirman & Dickson and Holcomb & Barnard. Within a month, however, most of the businesses were burned to the ground by retreating Confederate forces. *Courtesy Quintin Trammel.*

the battlefield for interment at Mount Comfort Cemetery. Members of the Masonic Lodge, of which Bell was a member, and a large number of residents escorted the soldiers' remains to the cemetery, where they were buried with honors. "The exercises were solemn and imposing; and the large concourse of citizens assembled showed the esteem in which the deceased patriots had been held by their fellow-citizens of Washington county."[52]

While the Missouri State Guard continued forays into Missouri to cause havoc, the mass of Confederate forces returned to Fayetteville and enlarged supplies at Fayetteville, using the building of the Northwestern Arkansas Baptist Female Institute on the northwest corner of College Avenue and Dickson Street as its arsenal. Confederate money had not made its way west yet, and local mercantiles began printing their own scrip at the beginning of 1862.

One of the Texans who came to Arkansas with McCulloch, John Henry Brown, retrieved a printing press from Springfield, Missouri; moved it into the courthouse at Fayetteville; and started publishing a newspaper called the *War Bulletin*. Brown, an early advocate of Texas secession, laid out the mission of the newspaper bluntly: "This sheet has nothing to do with local or State matters. The editor resides in Texas and is here, a stranger, to aid in the defence of constitutional Liberty against the mercenary minions of the child-murdering, woman-insulting, house-burning, negro-stealing, 'Bull-Run-'ing, infidel, Yankee nation—no more, no less."

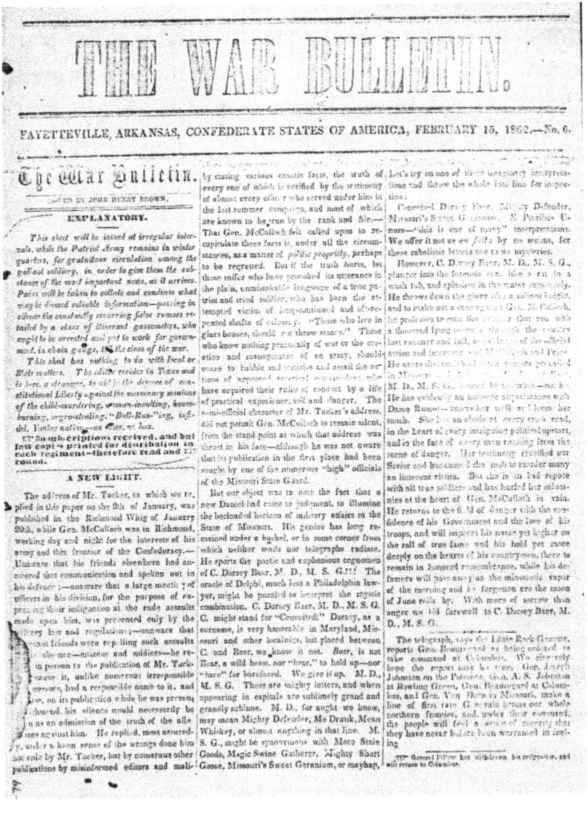

THE WAR BULLETIN.

FAYETTEVILLE, ARKANSAS, CONFEDERATE STATES OF AMERICA, FEBRUARY 15, 1862.—No. 6.

The War Bulletin.

ISSUED BY JOHN HENRY BROWN.

EXPLANATORY.

This sheet will be issued at irregular intervals, while the Patriot Army remains in winter quarters, for gratuitous circulation among the gallant soldiery, in order to give them the substance of the most important news, as it arrives. Pains will be taken to collate and condense what may be deemed reliable information—passing in silence the constantly recurring false rumors retailed by a class of itinerant gassonaders, who ought to be arrested and put to work for government, in chain gangs, till the close of the war.

This sheet has nothing to do with local or State matters. The editor resides in Texas and is here, a stranger, to aid in the defence of constitutional Liberty against the mercenary minions of the child-murdering, woman-insulting, house-burning, negro-stealing, "Bull-Run-"ing, infidel, Yankee nation—no more, no less.

No subscriptions received, and but few copies printed for distribution in each regiment—therefore read and pass round.

A NEW LIGHT.

After regular newspapers shut down during the Civil War, a Texan named John Henry Brown came to Fayetteville with General Benjamin McCulloch and began publishing a four-page paper intermittently in the county courthouse after Confederate troops removed a printing press from Springfield, Missouri, and hauled it to Fayetteville. Printing ended when Union forces marched south to Fayetteville in February 1862. *Courtesy UA Libraries.*

The paper issued only a half dozen editions through the late fall and winter of 1861–62, but it included news about troops encamped across Northwest Arkansas, a report of the running snowball fight among comrades at arms between the Butterfield House and the square and consistently more and more strident defenses of McCulloch, who was being criticized in Southern newspapers for not following up the victory at Wilson's Creek with a broader attack in Missouri to take it from the Federals.

Indeed, while the Confederates were engaging in snowball fights, the Union army was reorganizing and rebuilding under the leadership of General Samuel Curtis.

In early 1862, rumors swept through the town that Federal troops were moving south toward Arkansas, setting off a general exodus of residents trying to move their property and slaves to safer situations. One resident recalled, "About every one who could get away left Fayetteville at this time, and the line of carriages, wagons and horsemen must have been two miles or more long as they crossed the Boston mountains."[53]

In mid-February, the Union troops moved south to the Arkansas-Missouri border, and Confederate troops posted north of Fayetteville withdrew to the town. On February 25, General McCulloch ordered troops to move farther south beyond the Boston Mountains. He also ordered troops to burn all vacant buildings and any building or warehouse that might prove a military advantage to the Union. Merchants' buildings on the square were first to go, even those of merchants loyal to the Southern cause, and only a few brick buildings survived the conflagration, including Stephen Stone's store on the northeast side, the courthouse at the center and the Christian Church at the southwest corner. Soon, the steam mill in the Hollow and the old Butterfield stables along College Avenue were aflame.

Amid the general destruction, looting of stores and homes by soldiers and citizenry alike occurred. Reverend William Baxter recalled the desperate scene:

> *Whole companies would march out of town, each man with a ham, shoulder, or side of bacon on his bayonet, and no one could complain of them for thus wishing to change their camp fare but what could the others want with fine articles of ladies' wear, and, as I noticed in one case, a thermometer? Officers threatened, cursed, called them thieves, made appeals to their manliness and State pride, and to the fact that they were among those battling in the same cause; but all in vain; stealing had become a kind of recreation, and they would steal.*[54]

At the corner of College Avenue and Dickson Street, destruction of the Baptist Female Institute, which had been turned into an arsenal, was ordered. Baxter, who lived catty-corner across College Avenue from the Baptist Female Institute, told of one soldier riding up to the institute with orders to destroy it but being persuaded not to do so for the safety of nearby families:

> *Scarcely was he out of sight, when a few horsemen galloped up, entered the main building, and began to make preparation for burning it by pouring turpentine on the floors and between the ceilings; permission was asked to remove the bombshells, but they refused; the torch applied, and the flames spread so rapidly that the occupants of the next building had scarcely time to save their trunks and some bedding, before that was also on fire.*[55]

The fire reached the shells, and a "terrific explosion" within the building sent deadly fragments in all directions. Baxter's house soon caught fire as well, and he considered fleeing as another round of shells detonated. His wife convinced him that the worst might be past, and he and Robert Graham took to the roof of his house to subdue the flames. Not all residents were as fortunate: "When night fell a great portion of our town was a smoldering ruin."[56]

The Federal army entered the still-smoking ruins of Fayetteville, to the great acclaim of Union sympathizers.

The Battle of Pea Ridge and the Battle of Prairie Grove

The Union almost immediately withdrew from Fayetteville and returned to the Arkansas-Missouri border, establishing camps around a rocky eminence known as Pea Ridge. Within days, the Confederate army returned as a "living tide" that swept back over the Boston Mountains.

Reentering the town, General McCulloch ordered the arrest of Judge Jonas Tebbetts, who had the temerity to bring out a Union flag when the Federal troops had temporarily occupied Fayetteville. McCulloch sent Tebbetts to Fort Smith to await his return, at which time he was to be hanged as a traitor.

A few nights later, on March 4, Rebels burned the campus of Arkansas College before they moved out for battle with the Union. Early reports from the battlefield seemed to indicate a rout of the Union troops, although the reports were coming via Southern soldiers. As the two-day battle wore on, though, the reports coming into Fayetteville turned in nature. Soon the retreating Rebels, a "confused mob," gave evidence that the Union had been victorious. Generals McCulloch, McIntosh and Slack were dead; Louisiana's Colonel Louis Hébert and other senior officers had been captured. The commanding general, Earl Van Dorn, ordered retreat after realizing that his supply trains had accidentally been sent south. The Battle of Pea Ridge secured Missouri for the Union.

Throughout the rest of 1862, the Federal and Rebel armies played a game of cat and mouse across Northwest Arkansas and into the Indian Territory, but the cheese for the trap seemed to be Fayetteville. Whenever Union forces withdrew to Missouri, Confederate forces would occupy Fayetteville, and anytime the Union sent expeditions south, the Confederates removed south of the Boston Mountains:

> *The rebels are decidedly hard to catch. Notwithstanding our frequent night marches and forced marches in pursuit of them, we seem to be no nearer to bagging the game than we were a month ago. Last night General Schofield had accurate information that they were encamped, six or seven thousand strong, in the immediate vicinity of this place. In a few minutes the whole army was in motion, and great hopes were entertained that at last our chase was about to prove successful. We left Osage Springs just at dark, and by two o'clock in the morning were at Fayetteville....On arriving here everything was found perfectly quiet. The enemy's pickets were posted all around the town, but fled on our approach. Several shots were interchanged; but nobody was hurt....Last evening the town was in possession of the rebel army, and before daylight it was in possession of the Union army, and the change was effected so quietly that many citizens knew nothing about it until they saw the position of things this morning. They were utterly astonished.*

In the first week of December, though, the prey became the predator. The Union Army of the Frontier was divided into two parts, with half commanded by Brigadier General Francis Herron at Springfield, Missouri, and the other half commanded by Brigadier General James Blunt, who had orders to drive the Rebels out of Northwest Arkansas.

Confederate major general Thomas C. Hindman recognized that this split in the Union forces gave him an opportunity to strike full force at one half, defeat it and then take on the second. Colonel J.R. Pettigrew of Fayetteville recalled the morning that the Confederate troops left Fort Smith and massed at Lee Creek before marching north to engage the enemy:

> *No more impressive scene was ever witnessed in all this land than on that calm winter morning, to see thousands of soldiers kneeling with their faces northward, and the solemn invocation commending them and their fortunes to the arbitrament of arms and the God of battles. Thenceforth the red flag of battle waved over each command.*[57]

Part of Hindman's troops engaged Blunt and drew his forces deep into Arkansas with a series of battles near Cane Hill. Blunt held his troops at Cane Hill and fortified his position.

Hindman moved the main body of his troops north into Washington County, flanking Blunt and arriving at Prairie Grove. He initially thought that he would be able to attack Blunt unexpectedly but reconsidered because of the approach of Herron's troops from the north, which had performed a herculean forced march from Springfield to help Blunt, passing through Fayetteville during the night of December 6 and arriving on the battlefield early December 7.

Herron's artillery had range enough to begin taking out the Confederate artillery, but Hindman had an elevation advantage that allowed his troops to cut down advancing infantry. The sound of the battle could be heard easily at Fayetteville, but it also was heard by Blunt at Cane Hill, who put his troops in motion on double-quick toward the sound of battle. When they arrived, they attacked Hindman's left flank. The combined Union forces proved too much for Hindman to overcome. By the end of the day, the forces were at an effective stalemate, but Hindman withdrew from the field of battle during the night.

The wounded from the battle were brought to Fayetteville, where public buildings, schools and residences became hospitals for the more than 1,600 soldiers on both sides of the conflict. The town and surrounding region were not prepared for such a large number, and the mortality rate proved high among those severely wounded.

By the end of the year, Blunt and Herron had chased Hindman out of the Van Buren area. Union supporters in Fayetteville cheered the news. The *Boston Morning Journal* of Boston, Massachusetts, reported that "an enthusiastic Union demonstration occurred." Speeches were made by a Dr. Johnson, described as a prominent Union refugee, and Colonel Albert W. Bishop of the First Arkansas Cavalry, who served as provost marshal of the city at that time. According to the story, fifteen home guard companies were organized, and hundreds of citizens signed a petition to Congress requesting an election for a member of Congress from Arkansas.[58]

African American Self-Emancipation

Throughout the war, African Americans who had been enslaved in Fayetteville and across the region took steps to free themselves, stealing away during the moonless night or claiming refuge with Union troops as the troops moved north.

In one instance, a slave owner—fearing Union approach—determined to flee south with his belongings and sent a slave named John to get his mules and team harnessed for the journey. Some time passed without John returning, and the master, hearing that Federals were near, could wait no longer and departed in great haste, leaving John behind: "After a few days the Federal troops came in and John made his appearance, procured a wagon, put his baggage and his wife into it, and drove away, a happy fellow, when the army returned North again."[59]

Another slave, Dave Smith, escaped Fayetteville with the intention of finding freedom and fighting for the freedom of others. Smith's quest for "self-emancipation" came after an improbable journey that brought him to Fayetteville.

Dave Smith was born in the Cherokee Nation, probably in northern Georgia, to a Cherokee mother and an African father. His mother had purchased his father as a slave but then had also taken him as a husband. Because of the family situation, Dave and his sister grew up not realizing that their father was a slave nor understanding that in the eyes of Cherokee law they were slaves themselves. They did know something of hard fortune because they, like the rest of the Cherokees, had to forsake their home in 1838 when the U.S. government forced the Cherokees west to the Indian Territory.

After his mother died, however, he and his sister were placed in servitude, and he eventually was traded to a family named Tibets. Dave's son, Robert, later described his father's reaction to this turn of events:

> *My father was a big man, he weighed around 225 lbs. He had never been treated bad and it was purty hard for him to git used to being a slave. His master ordered him to be whupped and he wouldn't stand for it and he put up such a fight that they had him took to Fayettesville, Arkansas, and put in jail and held them there for sale. Didn't anybody want a big unruly ox…so he stayed in jail a long time.*[60]

Dave might have stayed in jail forever, but one day he overheard two other prisoners plotting. They wanted to overpower the sheriff, take his keys and escape. When the sheriff, Presley Smith, came into the jail to bring the inmates dinner, one of the outlaws knocked him down. Before the prisoners could go further, though, Dave waded into the fight, taking them by surprise, knocking them both out and preventing them from escaping or killing the sheriff. Impressed, the sheriff went right out, hunted up Dave's owner and paid him $600 for Dave.

Dave, who took his new master's surname, became a stonemason, and Presley Smith let him hire out for a variety of jobs around town, building stone foundations, rock walls and the like. He and another slave married, or "jumped the broom," as the custom was known among African Americans. They had several children and lived in the main house owned by Presley and Mary Smith. Dave Smith also took care of the yard, garden and barn, while his wife cooked for the household. Early in 1862, Presley Smith moved most of his slaves south to Texas, although Dave Smith remained in Fayetteville. By 1863, the Union army was occupying Fayetteville and controlling the rest of northern Arkansas. Dave Smith took his chance to leave. His son wrote, "My father and a lot more of the slaves of the neighbors around Fayettesville had slipped away and joined the northern army in Kansas. They belonged to the first and second Kansas regiment. They heard that if they would join up with the Yankees they would be set free so that's what they done."[61]

The First Regiment Kansas Volunteer Infantry (Colored) was organized at Fort Scott, Kansas, in early 1863, while the Second Regiment (Colored) was organized the following November. Both regiments served on the frontier and were the first African American troops to engage in battle on behalf of the United States of America. The regiments distinguished themselves in the Battle of Honey Springs in the Indian Territory, as well as during the Arkansas battles at Baxter Springs, Poison Springs and Jenkins Ferry. General James G. Blunt, who commanded Union troops engaged at the Battle of Honey Springs, later wrote, "I never saw such fighting as was done by the Negro regiment.…The question that negroes [*sic*] will fight is settled; besides they make better solders in every respect than any troops I have ever had under my command."[62]

After the war, Dave Smith lived in Lawrence, Kansas, where he died in 1867, a free man in a free nation.

Battle of Fayetteville

Since the Battle of Prairie Grove, Union troops had occupied Fayetteville and had driven Confederate troops beyond Van Buren on the Arkansas River Valley. During the months leading up to April, however, Confederate brigadier general William L. Cabell began amassing troops at Ozark, a situation apparent to the Union troops at Fayetteville. Cabell knew that the majority of Federal forces had withdrawn from Fayetteville, part for duty in southwest Missouri and part to serve in the Indian Territory.

Remaining at Fayetteville were the commanding officer, Colonel Marcus LaRue Harrison, and his regiment of the First Arkansas Cavalry. The Union troops also included a few companies of the Tenth Illinois Cavalry and the newly formed First Arkansas Infantry and First Light Artillery, which Harrison described in early April:

> *The First Arkansas Infantry will number in a few days an aggregate of 830 men, probably 700 of them effective. They are totally without transportation, clothing, or tents or equipments of any kind, except the arms picked upon the Prairie Grove battle ground, which are of all patterns and calibers. The destitution of clothing is very great, and much suffering prevails on account of it. Besides, it would be a ruinous policy to place this undrilled, barefooted, butternut regiment in the field to be mixed up with and cut in pieces by Rebels in the same dress. The First Arkansas Light Artillery numbers 110 men, who are destitute of clothing, and have never received their guns. Of course, nothing can be expected of them.*[63]

This was the force that Cabell expected to surprise and defeat. He was not shy about his next move. He issued special orders to enlist support of all troops in Northwest Arkansas "to rid that section of the state of the presence of an insolent and unscrupulous abolition invader."[64] By the time Cabell was ready to move north, he had nine hundred or so troops and hauled two six-pound howitzers along, knowing that the Union troops had no artillery.

Rather than follow the direct route from Ozark, Cabell took his troops west up the Arkansas River Valley to Frog Bayou and then north from there over the Boston Mountains, coming down the valley of the West Fork of the White River in the early morning hours of April 18. They hoped to catch the Union troops in Fayetteville by surprise but were surprised themselves when they reached the community of West Fork. They tumbled into a wedding party at a house with several Union soldiers, who were attending without permission and quickly became Cabell's first prisoners.

Cabell's troops continued to Fayetteville and arrived on the southern edge of the town just as light began to gather in the eastern sky. They veered northeasterly to take advantage of the Hollow splitting the Fayetteville Square from East Mountain, now known as Mount Sequoyah. Before gaining the Hollow, though, the Confederates were fired on by Federal soldiers on picket duty. The pickets were quickly overrun, but their shots gave warning

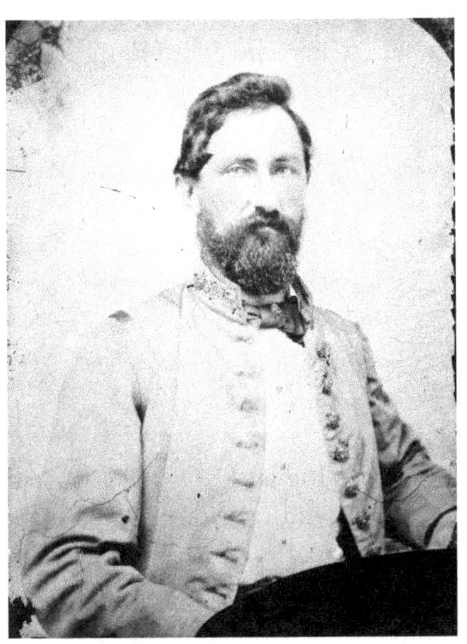

Brigadier General William Lewis Cabell, whose Confederate forces attacked Union troops occupying Fayetteville on April 18, 1863. *Courtesy Library of Congress Prints and Photographs Division, Brady-Handy Photograph Collection.*

to the Union headquarters. The Confederate troops pressed into the Hollow and up onto higher ground, looking for safe positions from which to engage the Yankees.

One of the Yankees, Lieutenant Elizur B. Harrison, the brother of Colonel Harrison, had taken up residence in the Baxter House at the corner of present-day College Avenue and Dickson Street. He awoke to an "unusual noise" out back. Putting on his clothes, he went to the back door to see what was happening. Between him and the Hollow was the enemy. Turning on his heels, he went out the front door as other civilian inmates of the house trundled downstairs into the presumed safety of the cellar. He circled north trying to get to the Union headquarters at the Tebbetts House but ran into his brother west of the house. They then ran north to the encampment of the First Arkansas Cavalry and the First Arkansas Infantry, which were quartered in tents on the block of land northwest of present-day College Avenue and Lafayette Street. Company officers were already rousting their troops to assembly. Harrison ordered most of the ill-equipped infantry to the far side of Mount Nord to keep them out of harm's way.[65]

Meanwhile, General Cabell followed his artillery up onto the southwestern flank of Mount Sequoyah, overlooking the entire town. He described the scene: "I found the enemy about 2,000 strong, well armed with Springfield and Whitney rifles, no artillery and nearly every hill dotted with rifle pits."[66]

The two howitzers began firing on the Union encampment, hastening some of the Federal soldiers toward safety beyond Mount Nord, while some three dozen broke rank and fled toward Missouri. Cabell, seeing confusion among the Union troops, ordered his dismounted cavalry soldiers to advance out of the Hollow, across William McGarrah's wheat fields and toward the Tebbetts and Baxter Houses. He then retrained the artillery on the Baxter House to drive Union soldiers away from it and allow his troops to advance.

Sarah Yeater; her son, Charley; and other civilians holed up in the cellar of the Baxter House for safety found it had its own risks:

> *Very soon after the first shots were fired a shell hit the jamb of the basement door, splintered it, knocked bricks from the chimney, broke a large kettle containing lye standing on the hearth, and rolled out of sight.... When my bedding was taken up, the shell, which failed to explode, rolled from it, and on examining my room in the cottage found that two bullets had passed through the mattress where Charley and I had been lying, the window and chamber set were broken and several bullets has passed through the walls.*[67]

In spite of another shell hitting and instantly killing James D. Bell, a private in Company I, the Union troops did not back down. Instead, they drove the Confederates back, using their longer-range Springfield and Whitney rifles against the short-range scatterguns of the Rebels. Colonel Harrison sent word to the Union left flank under charge of Lieutenant Colonel Albert Bishop to try to put pressure on the Confederate artillery, but the Texans defending that end of the battle line initially put up a stiff fight. Again, the firepower of the Union rifles drove them back, and soon the Union soldiers gained close enough vantage to shoot at the artillery battery. One of the Confederate gunners was hit and killed by the volley, while others were wounded. Rather than allow the artillery to fall into the hands of the enemy, Cabell ordered them withdrawn and sent south to the Arkansas River Valley. He also ordered a cavalry charge against the middle of the Union line at the intersection of College Avenue and Dickson Street. Union doctor Seymour Carpenter described the moment:

> *East of the road was a wide wooded ravine, in which, and screened by the timber, the enemy's cavalry formed for the charge. Suddenly I heard a tremendous yell, then the clatter of the horses, then the toss of their flags, and then they were upon us.... The brow of the hill was about 40 yards from the line. In a minute the long line of Cavalry appeared, the* [Union] *Major rushed in front, gave the command to fire, and a sheet of flame from five hundred carbines greeted them; dozens of men and horses went down; I could see the line waver, and the men frantically reining their horses, and swerving to the right and left. They were armed with sabres, and if they had pistols they did not use them. All our men had carbines and revolvers, and in a minute not a Rebel was in sight, save the killed and wounded.*

The cavalry charge proved an utter disaster, and Cabell ordered a withdrawal of troops:

> *After a furious fight of three hours and 10 minutes I withdrew my command in good order. I found it impossible with the arms I had, after my artillery ammunition was exhausted, to dislodge them from the houses and rifle pits with the kind of arms my command had without losing all my horses and a large number of my men, as it was impossible to get near enough to them to make our aim effective without a great sacrifice of life, much greater than would have been justifiable under the circumstances.*[68]

Historian Russell L. Mahan estimated that the Confederates suffered seventy killed or wounded and fifty-four captured. A minimum of eighteen soldiers were killed or mortally wounded. On the Union side, Mahan identified thirty-nine killed or wounded and ten captured, including one soldier who was hanged by the Confederates. Of the thirty-nine, a minimum of nine soldiers were killed or mortally wounded.[69]

Harrison's victory proved pyrrhic for Fayetteville. Not knowing Cabell's true plight—no forage for his horses, no food for his troops—Harrison decided that Fayetteville could not be defended and requested permission to withdraw his troops to Springfield, Missouri. When he pulled out, many of the residents who were sympathetic to the Union pulled out with him as well, heading north as refugees barely a week after the battle, seeking a safer place than the borderland of Arkansas and Missouri.

Another two weeks went by, and the Confederate partisans rode back into Fayetteville to occupy it for much of the summer. Colonel John Scott became commander of the Confederate troops headquartered at Fayetteville and established his headquarters at the Tebbetts House, the very same place Harrison had chosen when the Union controlled the town.

The Siege of Fayetteville

Union troops under Colonel Harrison returned to Fayetteville in the fall of 1863 and maintained a post through the remainder of the war. During 1864, a half dozen skirmishes were reported at Fayetteville and in the surrounding area. The rise of guerrilla operations that attacked isolated homesteads and farms across the region forced Harrison to adopt new defensive measures, including creation of post colonies. The colonies were farming collectives in which families willing to pledge loyalty to the Union would live, work and be protected together. They would be provided between one thousand and four thousand acres of farmland.[70]

Likewise, Harrison had erected breastworks around downtown Fayetteville and extended the rifle pits into a network of trenches to aid in defense of the town. On October 25, 1864, his defensive position got a test from Colonel William Brooks, whose Confederate troops attacked the town.

Brooks declared that the Union forces would have neither forage for their animals nor subsistence for their men within the fortified barricades. One writer described the situation inside the Fayetteville garrison: "By good fortune we had twenty days and one quarter rations on hand, and, therefore, were in no trouble on this score, well knowing that ere it was exhausted, Price's campaign must be ended and our pressure relieved. In the matter of forage, papers were tight. We had but two hundred horses and could not send out a train. To do so was to ensure its capture."[71] Instead, Colonel Harrison furnished each mounted soldier with a sack and sent them galloping through the enemy lines to gather forage from farms outside the besieged town. Brooks's troops were spread thin on the perimeter of the town, and this tactic worked for the most part, although one foray faced a running battle for nearly five miles while trying to return to its garrison.

While this standoff occurred in Fayetteville, Confederate general Sterling Price returned from his mad dash into Missouri as far north as Lexington. After his troops caused as much havoc in Missouri as they could, they retreated down the western side of Missouri and reached Arkansas at the beginning of November. Brooks sent an appeal for reinforcements to break the back of the Union defense. Price reported, "Information was received by General Fagan from Colonel Brooks that he had the town of Fayetteville, Arkansas, closely invested, having forced the garrison within their fortifications, and asking for men to enable him to take it. As this was a place of importance to the Federals, and its capture would be of great advantage to the cause, upon General Fagan's earnest solicitation, I ordered a detail of five hundred men and two guns to be made to him for that purpose."[72] Reports from Colonel Harrison put the number of Rebel troops besieging Fayetteville as high as eight thousand.[73]

On November 3, Fagan's troops and two artillery pieces joined Brooks, and together they renewed the attack. The artillery pieces were set on a hilltop farm northwest of town, the present-day campus of the University of Arkansas, and the Confederate cavalry and infantry moved to attack from the north side of town. The Union troops prepared for the brunt:

> *At 10:30 A.M. they drove in our pickets, and at 11, opened with two guns well served, on our earth-works, at the same time deploying heavy lines on the south and left of us, gradually extending their lines on the north. At noon they had massed an attacking column on the north, and soon attempted to deploy and dress a line to charge the works. In this they were completely foiled by our sharpshooters in the rifle pits* [who] *threw so close and deadly fire among them that the men would not come to time—three times more they made the attempt and each time failed most signally.*[74]

The shelling continued from 11:00 a.m. until sunset. Anticipating that the artillery would eventually force the Union forces to flee the downtown fortification, Fagan left the eastern side of the town seemingly unguarded. However, he surreptitiously sent cavalry to the Hollow on the east side with orders to "remain in the saddle and to charge the Feds, the moment they reach you in their retreat."

A Federal retreat never came. The Union troops could not be dislodged. Neither the repeated Rebel charges nor the incessant artillery shelling could unsettle the Union troops, who remained cool behind their breastworks and within their trenches. As night fell, Fagan ordered his troops to begin withdrawing toward Cane Hill to rejoin Price, staying one step ahead of the approach of the U.S. Army of the Border, which had chased Price out of Missouri. Fagan left about six hundred to resume the shelling on the morning of November 4, but even they decamped when scouts warned of the approaching Union army.

One of the advancing Union troops coming out of Missouri wrote of their early morning sojourn:

> *At three o'clock on the morning of the fourth, the camp was aroused by the shrill notes of the bugle sounding the assembly and in one hour's time, the command was moving forward in the direction of Fayetteville.... The storm had now abated, although it was yet stinging cold, and the command pushed forward as fast as the condition of the roads and the jaded stock would admit of, to relieve the heroic garrison from the attack of five times their number, assisted by two pieces of artillery.... The command reached Fayetteville at 11 o'clock, the rebels having abandoned the siege, three hours' previous. The garrison and the citizens of the town were necessarily*

> *frightened at the unexpected appearance of such a large force of the enemy, and were greatly relieved upon witnessing our approach.*[75]

Both troops and civilians survived the onslaught without significant casualty. The same could not be said for many of the residences. Damage from one of the shells is still visible on the western wall of the Walker-Stone House on Center Street. Other houses were more heavily damaged:

> *One conspicuous house, into the cellar of which was congregated fifty or sixty women and children, was completely riddled; five shells have passed directly through it, and one of them exploding in the kitchen shattered the walls in a frightful manner. A solid shot fired at this house passed through the hewed-log walls and striking a mule killed it instantly.*[76]

The twelve-day siege was lifted and proved to be the last major engagement between Union and Confederate forces in Fayetteville. The Union troops continued their chase of Price south to Van Buren and across the Arkansas River. Several days later, Abraham Lincoln was reelected

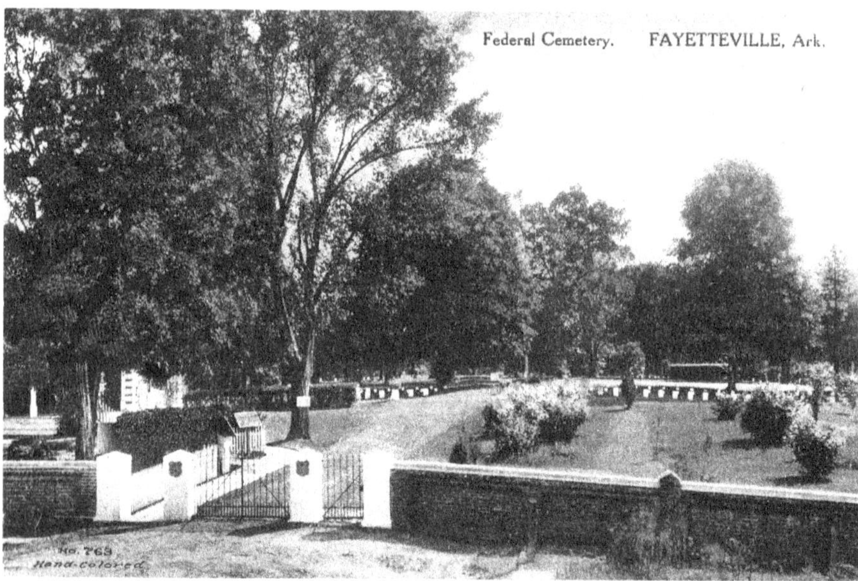

Fayetteville National Cemetery was approved in 1867, and it was established on a small knoll of land earlier known as Gallows Hill. Initially, the remains of Union soldiers were disinterred from battlefields in Northwest Arkansas and reinterred at the cemetery. Today, the cemetery is the final resting place for veterans from every American war, including the Revolution. *Author's collection.*

president of the United States. In the spring of 1865, Union successes in the eastern United States forced the surrender by General Robert E. Lee to General Ulysses S. Grant. Other Confederate generals followed suit, the last being tendered by General Stand Waite of the Cherokee Confederate troops in the Indian Territory.

After the war, in 1867, National Cemetery was established on the south side of Fayetteville as a final resting place for Union soldiers who had fought and died in Northwest Arkansas. Today, veterans of every American war, from the American Revolution to the wars against Afghanistan and Iraq, are buried at the cemetery.

In 1872, a group of Fayetteville women met at the Methodist church and organized the Southern Memorial Association to secure a site for proper burial of Confederate soldiers who had lost their lives in Northwest Arkansas battles. The Confederate Cemetery was established on three acres near the eastern end of Rock Street. Soldiers from battles across Northwest Arkansas were reinterred there. Today, the association continues to maintain the cemetery.

CHAPTER 4

RECONSTRUCTION AND THE END OF THE WILD WEST

Between the end of the Civil War and the turn of the twentieth century, Fayetteville faced many of the same problems as Arkansas and the South. The period of Reconstruction was more than a physical rebuilding of destroyed cities and farms. It meant a resurrection of polity, of civic institutions and cultural accommodation in ways that had not been acceptable prior to the war and that were exacerbated by the war. Much of Fayetteville had been laid waste by the end of the war. Residents had fled south and north depending on their proclivities, and many did not return, particularly those sympathetic to the North. The 1860s proved to be the only decade in which Fayetteville lost population between the decennial censuses.

By 1868, though, the town was strongly on the mend. New mills, dry goods stores, mercantiles, a "fashionable millinery and dress making establishment," a sash-and-door manufactory, dentists, doctors, ophthalmologists, a photographer and a variety of saloons with billiards and even bowling were all advertised in the local paper. The Fayetteville market had flour, corn by the bushel, hams, bacon, butter, eggs, apples, lard, chickens, coffee, sugar and molasses for sale, all the staples that could not be had for a king's ransom during the war. Livery stables and stage routes were reopened. Perhaps no greater evidence of the town's rebound could be found than a report that U.S. soldiers stationed at Fayetteville had formed the Primitive Base Ball Club and announced that they would play Fayetteville's Urban Club, inviting the townspeople

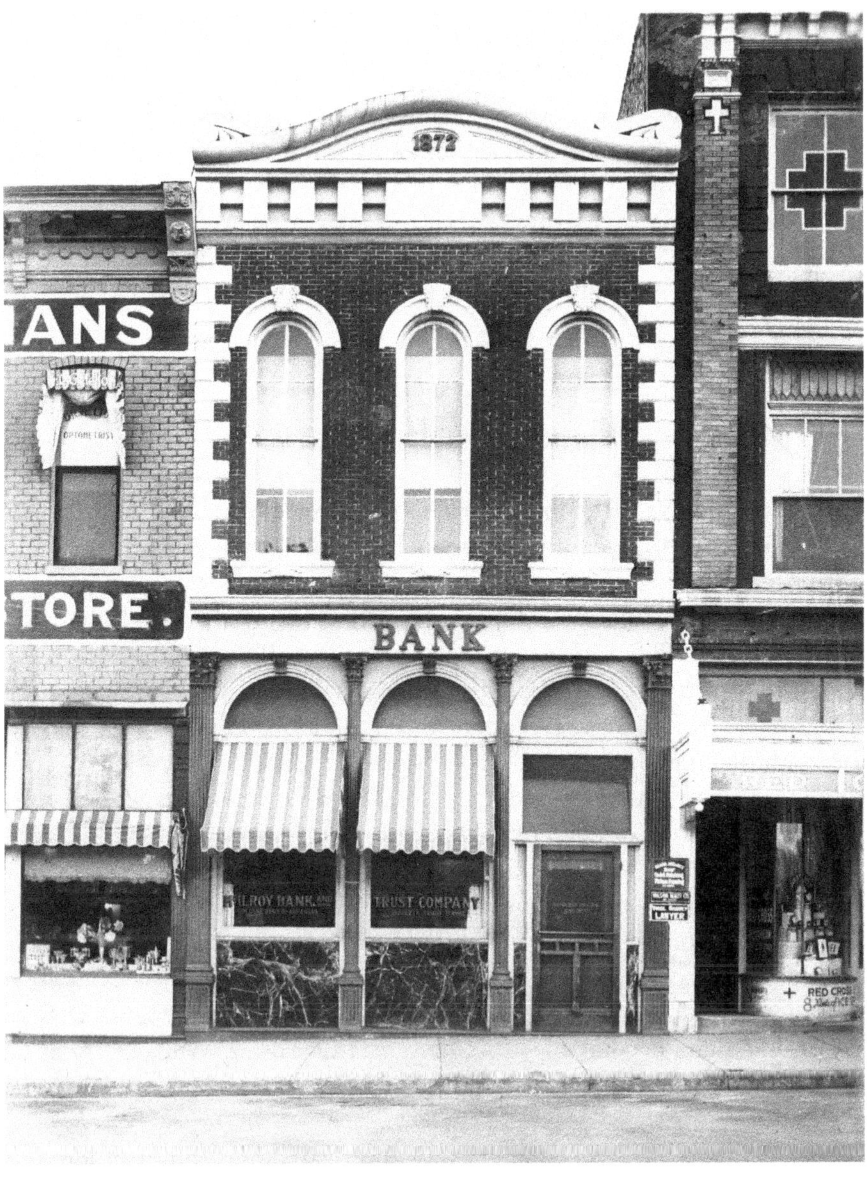

McIlroy Bank and Trust on the Fayetteville Square was chartered in 1871 and began operation in 1872. It came fully under the guiding hand of William McIlroy after his partner, Denton Stark, fled the town in 1875 following the discovery that he had overextended his finances. McIlroy continued to operate on the Fayetteville Square until 1986, when the bank was purchased by Arvest Bank. *Courtesy UA Libraries, McIlroy Bank Collection, MC890.*

to see the contest, which was scheduled the same day as the Slow Mule Race: "We would be especially delighted to see a goodly number of the fair ones present, to who we give the assurance that nothing will be said or done that could in any manner offend the most fastidious."[77]

As with its initial growth, civic leaders turned to development of educational facilities. Within a little over three years, Fayetteville had established a public school for African American youth, a public school district for European American youth and the state's first public university.

Former Foes Join Education Effort

After the Civil War, Republicans took control of government in Arkansas and promised to develop a public school system. They proposed legislation for primary and secondary schools, as well as for a state university. At the same time, Ebeneazor Enskia Henderson moved from Indiana to Fayetteville in 1866 and began making good on that promise. He came to Fayetteville as a teacher for the American Missionary Society and the U.S. Bureau of Refugees, Freedmen and Abandoned Lands, and he helped establish the first public school in the state.[78]

Land was purchased for one dollar from Lafayette and Mary Gregg near the present-day intersection of Olive Avenue and Sutton Street, and a two-room brick school was built for education of the sons and daughters of African American residents, most of them recently emancipated by the war. Clara Henderson, the daughter of E.E. Henderson, also served as one of the school's first teachers.[79]

Other teachers at Henderson included Dora Ford, Washington Pendar, S.H. Hill, Beulah Challelle, B.F. Foster, H.D. Foster, Willis Polk, Susie Pettigrew, H.L. Bird, Lucille Ingram, Herman Caldwell and Minnie Caldwell.

The ethnicity of early teachers was European American, and some of them were not accepted by the majority European American community in Fayetteville. E.E. Henderson reported that Ford "is totally ostracized from society, and that opposition to the erection of the bureau school house there is so bitter as to alarm the contractors."[80] Educator F.S. Root speculated that this was caused in part because the teachers at Henderson were paid with legal currency, while teachers at the other public schools were paid with scrip, which was often discounted 25 to 30 percent. But

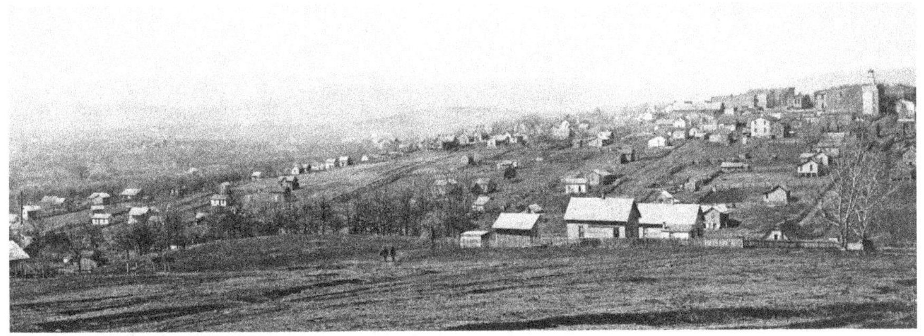

A panoramic photo shows south Fayetteville in about 1890 from the southwestern flank of Mount Sequoyah. After the Civil War, much of the town was denuded of trees. The building with the cupola at right is the old county courthouse, which stood at the center of the Fayetteville Square. *Author's collection.*

Root also acknowledged the lingering prejudices wrought by the war against educators from the North or East Coast.[81]

The American Missionary Association funded the operations of the school during its first years but had to withdraw financial support for a period after it sustained a drop in its own resources in the 1870s. The society and the Fayetteville School Board probably provided joint support until the school board purchased the Mission School property for $500 in 1894 and added an annex to the original building.

By 1885, the school district listed 139 students attending the Mission School.[82]

In 1889, the school board voted to name the school in honor of E.E. and Clara Henderson at the same time that it named the other two grade schools in honor of George Washington and Thomas Jefferson. In 1910, the U.S. Census listed Fayetteville as having fifty African American children of school age, and forty-four of them were attending school.[83]

Between 1910 and 1917, enrollment of African American students countywide dropped from 215 students in 1910 to 150 in 1915 and then 111 by 1917. The 1917 figure represented about one-third of the African American children of school age, according to the county board of education. The high percentage of students not enrolled might reflect the county's lack of schools for African American students outside Fayetteville, but the general drop also demonstrated an outmigration of African American families from Washington County that started in 1890.[84]

During the 1920s and early 1930s, the Parent-Teacher Association became active, and programming at Henderson grew beyond the normal

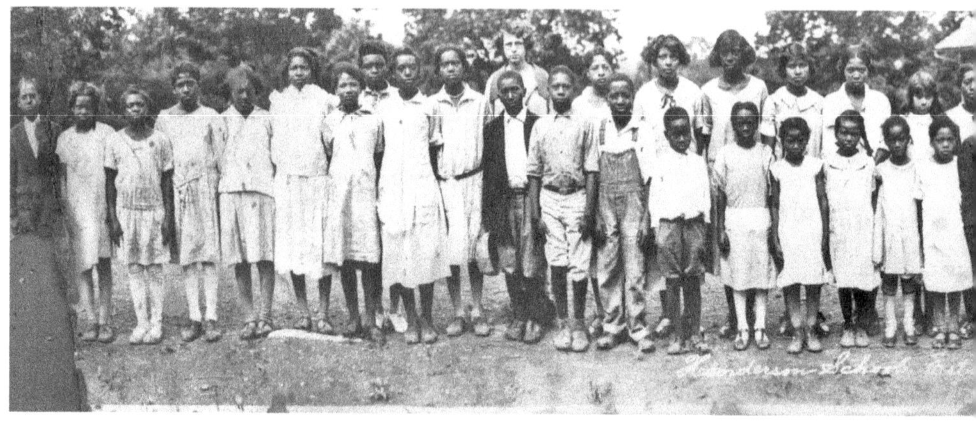

curriculum to include special events and projects. In 1936, for instance, Henderson School included a health program as part of Negro Health Week and then a "book shower" to celebrate the creation of the George Ballard Memorial Library as part of National Library Week. In the latter case, the district superintendent, F.S. Root, introduced Ballard and Herman Caldwell, principal of the school, and then heard from Harry Dane, who had traveled around the world twice, and Rosa Marinoni, who read some of her poetry. Entertainment was provided by Frank Owens and his Ginger Band, as well as a tap dance by Half-Pint Thompson.

In an interview, Betty Hayes Davis recalled starting school at Henderson when she was six years old. Her family lived on Olive Avenue close to the two-room school:

> *The bell would ring, and I would start sprinting and get in line. We always had to line up to go into school. And I was only about a half block away. Living so close, I didn't think I needed to take a note for being late. I just liked the idea of hearing that bell and knowing, whoops, I got to go! Be there in time to get in line and march into school. At Henderson, you went from one room to the other, depending on what grade you were in. One room would simply change classes by the front row going to the back. Sometimes, depending on what grade you were in, you might have gone from one room to the other. It was just shifting between those two rooms for eight grades.*

In 1934, as a project of the Federal Emergency Relief Administration during the Depression, ten African American men were hired to disassemble the first Jefferson School and remove the building materials for use in building a new school for African American students at the southeast corner of Willow

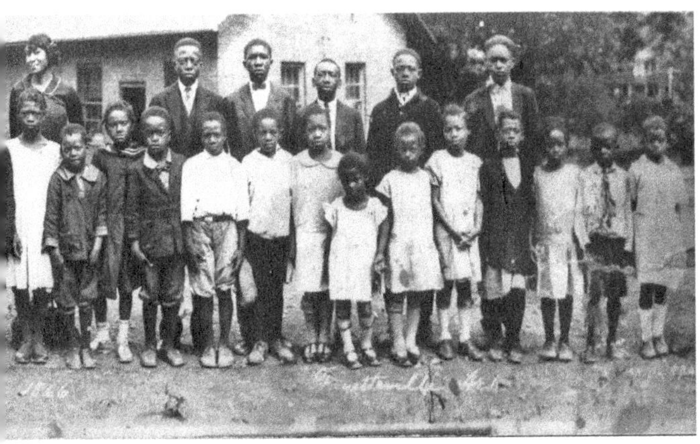

Students of Henderson School pose for a class picture in 1926, with the school in the background. Henderson was the first public school chartered by Arkansas in 1866 and was operated until 1936, when Lincoln School opened for African American students. *Courtesy Betty Hayes Davis.*

Avenue and Center Street. The new school was finished by 1936 and included three rooms plus a full basement. The school district named it Lincoln School and valued the building at $20,000.[85]

Davis recalled making the switch from Henderson up on the hill to Lincoln down in the Hollow:

> *We marched to that building. We marched and we sang. The principal's wife, who taught also in that school—she was a music major—and she wrote this song for us to sing:*
>
> *"Old Henderson School is too old for its age,*
> *Since the new Lincoln was built.*
> *Old Henderson School is just too old for its age,*
> *Since new Lincoln was built.*
> *Seventy years without stumbling, tick, tock, tick, tock.*
> *It's lights never trembling, don't stop, don't stop.*
> *But it's closed now, never to open again,*
> *Since the new Lincoln was built."*[86]

The opening of Lincoln School continued to provide students greater opportunities for learning beyond the normal curriculum. In 1938, for instance, the seventh- and eighth-grade classes learned about fire prevention. Principal Herman Caldwell said that the students collected newspaper stories about fires and learned about the danger of fires started in dry forests.

Minnie Dawkins became principal in 1946 and led the school until 1959. She "maintained a constantly changing flow of activities, managing

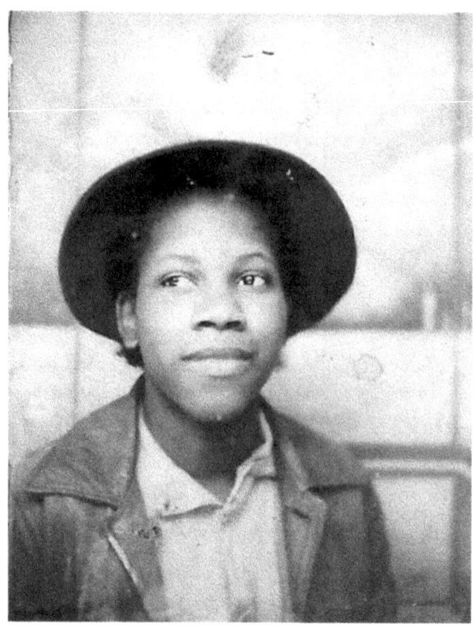

Betty Hayes attended Henderson School as a young girl and, along with other students, made the transition to Lincoln School when it opened in 1936. *Courtesy Betty Hayes Davis.*

recitation in a way that kept students engaged. She created uncertainty by calling on students randomly and they had to be prepared to respond."[87]

Lincoln School remained in operation until the early 1960s, when the school district was integrated. The school district integrated slowly, starting with the high school students, as the district didn't offer high school instruction for African American students prior to integration. Then they worked down to junior high and eventually the grade schools, phasing out Lincoln School at the end of the process. Among the last teachers at Lincoln, Romey and Thelma Thomason moved to other Fayetteville schools as administrative integration finished.[88]

Following the establishment of Henderson School, a public school board was established in 1871 to oversee the public education of European American students in schools separated from the African American students. Immediately after the Civil War, most of the European American students were being taught in private or subscription schools offered by local teachers. The first public classes were held in churches, the Masonic Hall and private homes. With the opening of the Arkansas Industrial University in 1872, Fayetteville families who could afford to do so also enrolled their children in the Preparatory Department created by the university.

More than a decade passed before voters approved a millage tax of ten mills in 1884 to be levied for the public school system. Half of the revenues went to a building fund, and half were used for all teaching purposes. The board contracted with Albert M. Byrnes to build the town's first public school for European American students. It was called North School originally but was renamed Washington School in 1889. It stood on the grounds of the present-day Washington Elementary.

In 1885, the board stated, "We report one school-house built during the year. Its foundation is stone; its walls, brick; its roof, iron; contains two large halls, and six good class rooms; material and finish, good; location, on an eminence in a seven-acre lot; cost of buildings and grounds, about $9,131.55."[89]

Within five years, the popularity of the public school had encouraged the school board to erect a second school, initially known as South School and renamed Jefferson School in 1889. It stood at the southeast corner of Church Avenue and South Street. By the end of the century, residential growth north of the university campus necessitated a third primary school, named after the Leverett family and erected at the northeast corner of Garland Avenue and Maple Street. Both Jefferson and Leverett Schools were eventually moved to different locations with larger school buildings.

At the state level, the Arkansas legislature finally approved the founding of the state's first university in 1871. A board of trustees was appointed, and it sought bids from communities from across the state for a site for the new university, to be called the Arkansas Industrial University. Fayetteville residents, recognizing the great value that Arkansas College and the Fayetteville Female Seminary had contributed to the town,

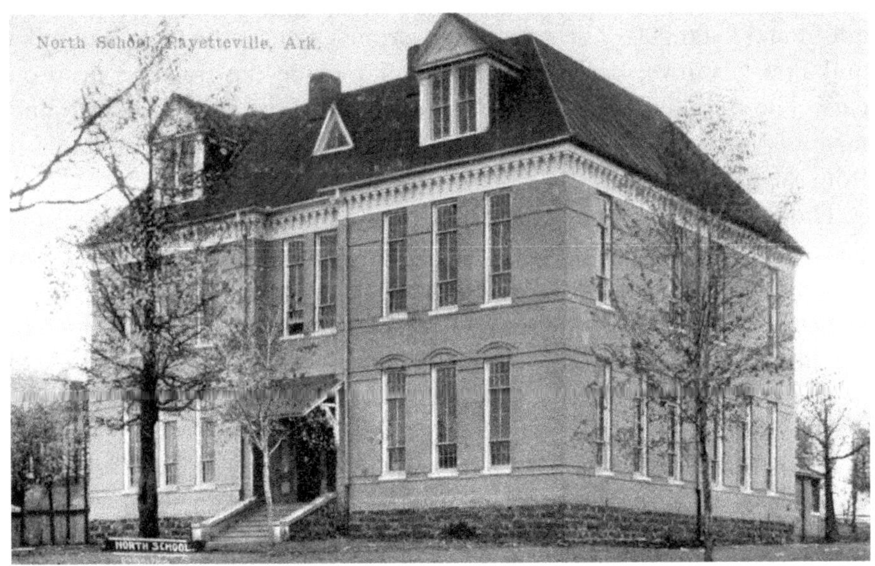

The first public school built for European American students was North School, built in 1885 on the site of the present-day Washington Elementary School. South School was built six years later at the corner of Church and South Streets. *Author's collection.*

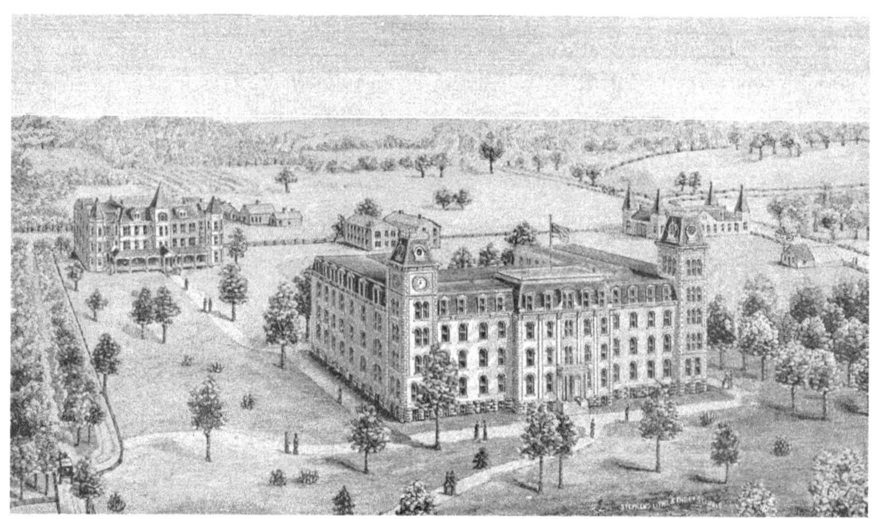

A lithograph depicts the Arkansas Industrial University campus, later renamed the University of Arkansas. In addition to Old Main, the campus included Buchanan Hall to the left and the Agricultural Experiment Station to the upper right.

were determined to win the bid. The city offered $30,000 in bonds and more than four hundred acres of land. Washington County offered an additional $100,000. The only other serious offers came from Batesville and Prairie Grove, but Fayetteville's offer made the trustees' decision easy. The Buildings and Grounds Committee chose the homestead and farm of William McIlroy as site of the new university and purchased it from the McIlroy family.

Though foes during the war, David Walker and Lafayette Gregg came together as colleagues to ensure that the university was built. The first classes were held in a frame building hastily erected to meet the deadline of the Morrill Land Grant Act. Eight students matriculated on the first day, January 22, 1872. By the fall of 1872, hundreds of students were enrolled, most of them being assigned to the Preparatory Department because very few had had sufficient schooling during the war period.

By 1875, the main building of the university, now known as Old Main, was finished. Designed in the Second Empire style by Chicago architect John Van Osdel, its two towers stood high above the tree line and could be observed from all entrances to Fayetteville. Today, the building remains a primary academic building and is a symbol of higher education in Arkansas.

The history of the university, which became known as the Hill, is well documented in other books, but its affect on Fayetteville has been profound. The hundreds of students in its early days and the tens of thousands of students arriving by the twenty-first century generated an enormous economy, from retail purchases made directly by students to the hospitality industry serving Razorback fans each fall and the housing market catering to students, staff and faculty. The insular nature of the university economy has tended to help the city weather downturns in the national economy.

Likewise, the constant roil of new students each year and the intermittent swirl of new faculty have also forced Fayetteville residents to recognize and embrace change as a constant. New ideas, new theories and new ways of looking at the world run like rivulets off the Hill and into the minds of Fayetteville's best and brightest.

The Railroad Arrives

Soon after the Civil War, residents of Northwest Arkansas began agitating for construction of a railroad through the region. The St. Louis & San Francisco Railway, better known as the Frisco—which operated lines out of St. Louis southwest through Springfield, Missouri, and into Oklahoma—was looking for a direct route to Paris, Texas. In 1881, the railroad company began building south from Monette, Missouri, and reached Fayetteville on June 8, 1881, where one of the largest crowds assembled greeted the president of the line. The easiest part of the route was done, and it would take another year to reach Fort Smith. The first regularly scheduled passenger train arrived on July 4, 1882. Aboard was an eleven-year-old boy named Willie Swaney, getting his first wide-eyed ride into Fayetteville and finding a crowd of ten thousand people awaiting, five times the population of the town.[90]

Although passenger trains fulfilled the desire of residents for easy transportation into and out of Fayetteville, the real lifeblood of the railroad were the freight trains that brought goods and resources into the town and then departed with produce and manufactured goods for sale in markets one thousand miles away. Hoppers, gondolas and boxcars brought sand, gravel and Texas beef into town; flatbeds, tankers and reefer cars carried away lumber, furniture, dairy products and barrels of apples, peaches and pears bound for the urban markets of the upper Midwest.

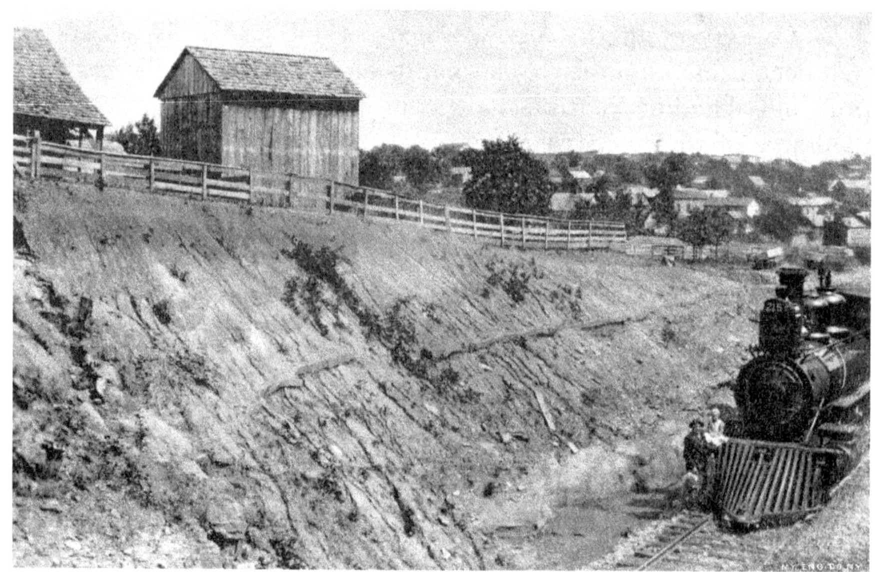

Frisco Engine no. 215 waits at the north end of the Fayetteville railroad yard near where the present-day Lafayette Street bridge crosses the railroad. On the horizon, the cupola of the Washington County Courthouse stands above the center of the Fayetteville Square in this circa 1888 photo published in the *Annual Report of the Geological Survey of Arkansas, for 1888.*

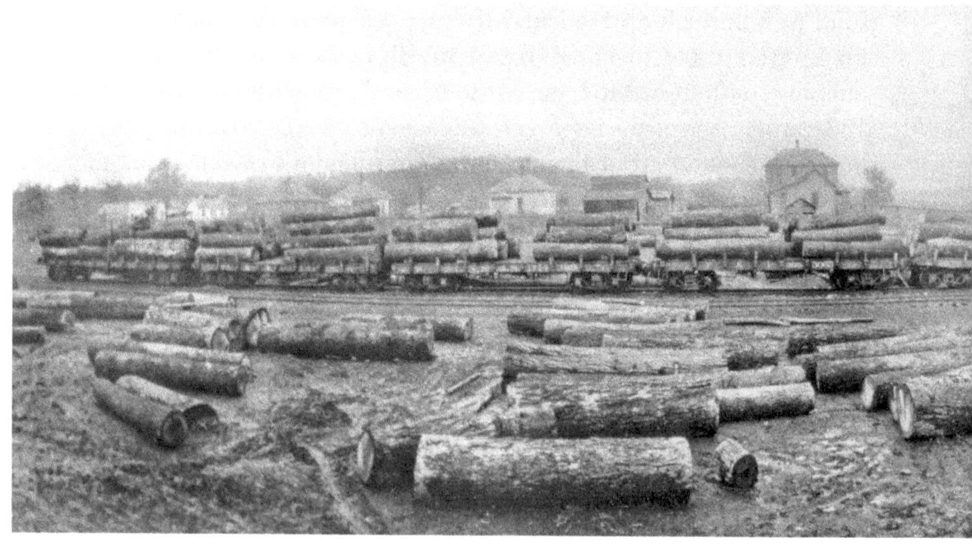

Fayetteville became a hub for other lines spurring off the Frisco main line. The hardwoods of the Ozarks to the east, the nascent fruit industry to the west of Fayetteville and the ever-promoted hope of being linked into a transcontinental line prompted organization of four lines that built out of Fayetteville.

Years before the Frisco reached Fayetteville, investors began planning an east–west rail line with Fayetteville as its center point. The resulting Pacific & Great Eastern Railway Company was incorporated in 1884, and a route was selected that swept around the south side of Fayetteville and headed toward the Wyman community east of Fayetteville. Twelve miles of the road were constructed by 1885 to Wyman, but the P&GE capital was not enough to continue construction further. The line continued for some years, with mixed freight and passenger service to the end of line, where passengers could take a swim in the White River.

In 1886, articles of association were filed to create the Fayetteville & Little Rock Railroad Company. The projected route of the rail line would run east up the valley of the White River to St. Paul and then south to Lewisburg in Conway County. The route did indeed get built as far as St. Paul, extending slightly farther to Pettigrew, and a spur known as the Cass & Black Mountain Railroad was built up over the Boston Mountains and back down almost to Cass. These two lines were used to transport timber from the heart of the

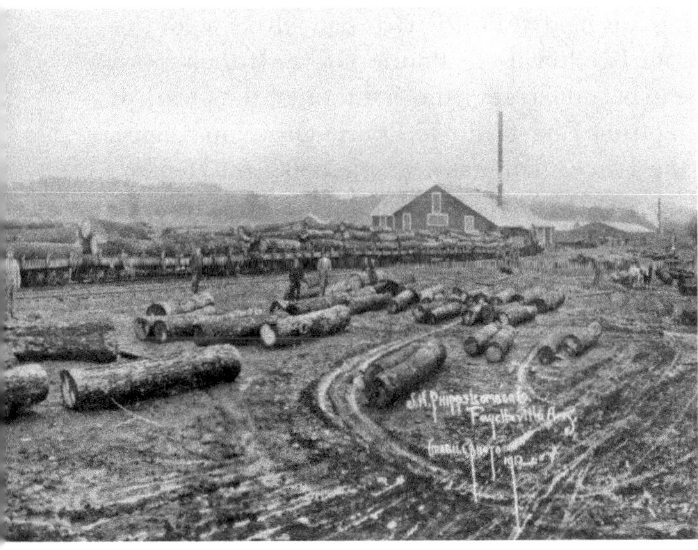

A log train waits at J.H. Phipps Lumber Company on the southwest side of Fayetteville in 1912. *Photograph by Burch Grabill. Courtesy Shiloh Museum of Ozark History, Robert Saunders Collection: S-96-2-542.*

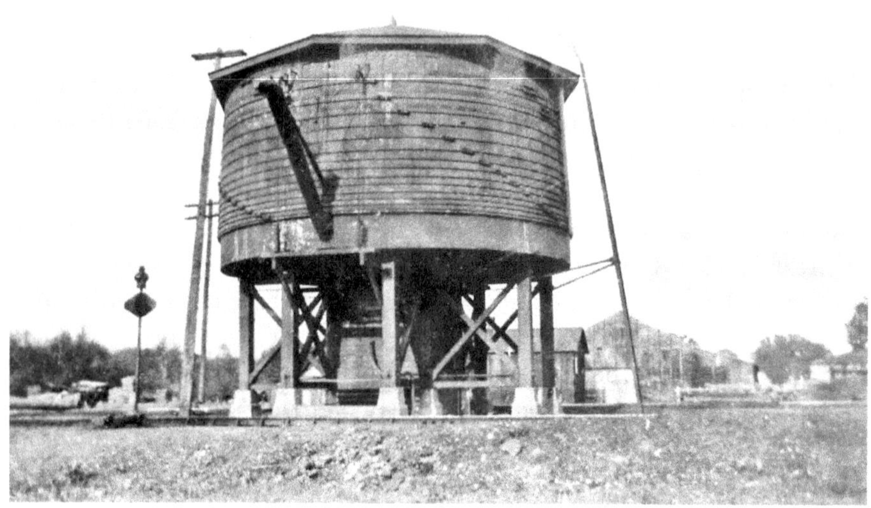

A Frisco Railroad water tank at Fayette Junction on the south side of Fayetteville, as photographed in the 1910s. Fayette Junction connected the St. Paul Branch with the main Frisco line. *Courtesy Shiloh Museum of Ozark History, Virginia Threet Collection, S-88-156-1.*

upland Ozark forest back to Fayetteville, where it could be milled for use as railroad ties, building lumber, barrel staves and wagon parts, among other uses. This line became known locally as the St. Paul Branch.[91]

In 1888, a mass meeting was held at Prairie Grove to advocate for the construction of a line from Fayetteville to Prairie Grove. It took more than a decade for the line to become reality, the first train of the Ozark & Cherokee Central running from Fayetteville to Prairie Grove on August 22, 1901. The line left the Frisco mainline near the depot on Dickson Street and then stayed east of the mainline, paralleling West Avenue before bending west just south of present-day Martin Luther King Boulevard; then it paralleled MLK to Farmington, Prairie Grove, Lincoln and Summers, eventually extending to Tahlequah and Okmulgee in the Indian Territory. A small depot for the O&CC was built about where the Farmers Coop sits today.

In 1891, Arkansas senator John Tillman of Fayetteville introduced the state's first "Jim Crow" legislation during the General Assembly. His law required citizens of African American heritage who are traveling by railroad to sit only in designated cars. Similar legislation over the next two decades would lead to racial segregation of most public buildings and institutions.

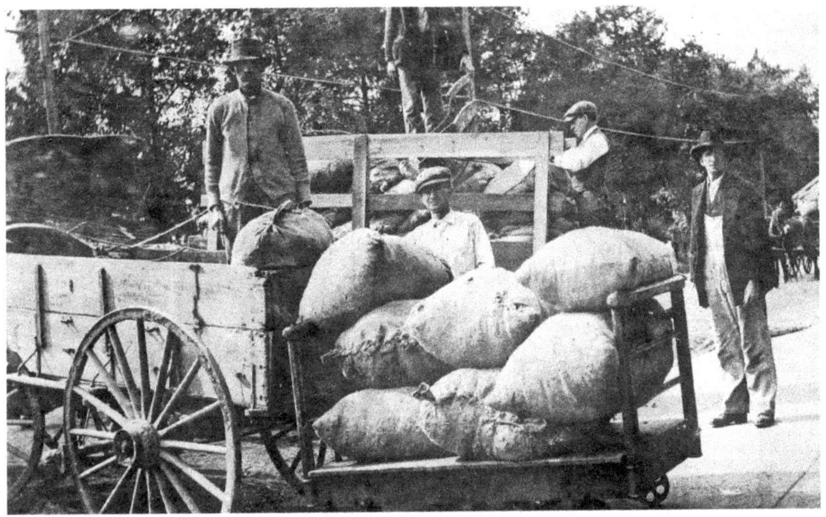

Farmers bring apples to the A.C. Hamilton warehouse on Center Street for sale during the first decade of the nineteenth century. The apple industry across Northwest Arkansas led to a variety of apple manufacturing operations, from further processing into ciders and dried apples to supporting industry such as barrel and stave makers. *Courtesy UA Libraries, William S. Campbell Collection, MC1427.*

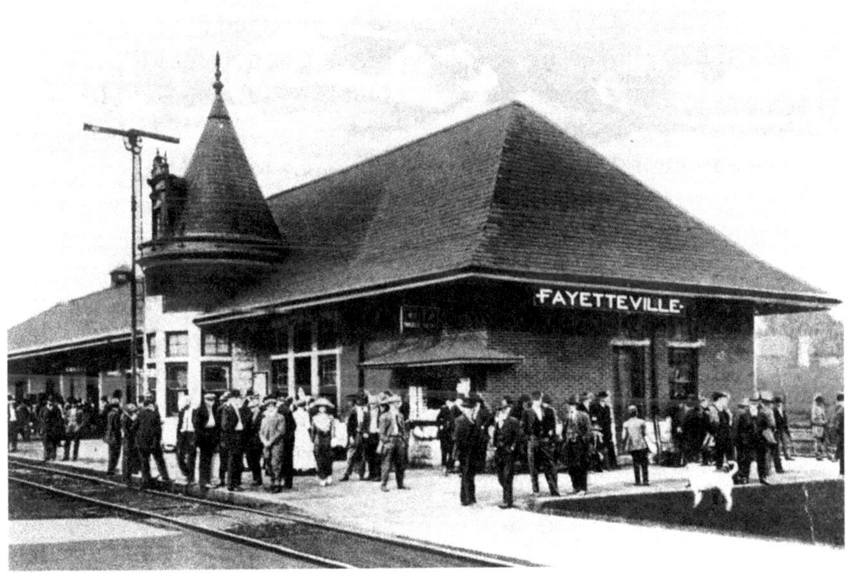

The Fayetteville Railroad Depot proved to be a popular spot when this photo was take in about 1915. This depot was the second of three on this site and was replaced by the current depot in 1925. The current depot and transfer building have been converted into restaurants, so they remain popular spots. *Courtesy Gresham, UA Libraries, Kent Brown Collection, M475.*

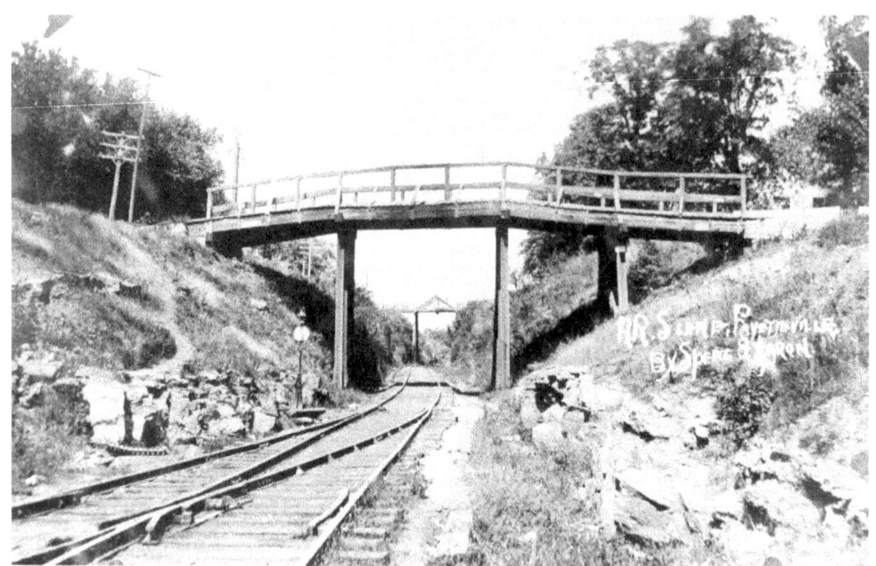

The Frisco Cut, with an early wooden Lafayette Street bridge in the foreground and the Maple Street bridge in the background, in about 1909. The two bridges were replaced with concrete bridges that are now in the National Register of Historic Places. *Photo by Speece & Aaron. Courtesy Shiloh Museum of Ozark History, Mrs. Kenneth Tillotson Collection, S-90-91-1.*

In 1903, the O&CC received permission to extend its line another four hundred miles, purchasing the Shawnee, Oklahoma and Missouri line in the Indian Territory, adding a connection from Okmulgee to Muskogee. The railroad also made plans to build east in Arkansas to Jasper, Newton County, although this latter project never came to fruition.[92]

The short-lived Kansas City & Memphis—the track of which never left Washington and Benton Counties in Arkansas—was the last line built out of Fayetteville, connecting the town with Mount Comfort, the Steele community, Litteral, Tontitown, Elm Springs and Cave Springs. Promoted as the "Fruit Belt Line," the KC&M intended to gather produce such as strawberries at each community for shipping at either end of the line. It was not uncommon for the train to stop and wait for its cargo if pickers were still in the field gathering the freshest fruit. The line went into receivership two years later but continued operation until World War I, when it was abandoned.

Over the course of the early part of the twentieth century, these additional lines played out their financial usefulness and were closed one by one. In 1965, Frisco announced it would curtail its passenger service to Fayetteville. On the evening of September 17, 1865, the last northbound passenger train pulled out of Fayetteville. The Hillcrest Junior High Band played, and the brick platform overflowed with a sentimental crowd. In the early morning hours of the next day, the last southbound passenger train, the so-called Cannonball, pulled out with less fanfare: "Engineer M.E. Brewster throttled his big diesel toward its final stop in Fort Smith just a little more than 83 years and two months after the first passenger train whistled its way into Fayetteville on a hot Fourth of July in 1882.... The final train drew eight people, most of them railroad fans."[93]

Conductor Hugh Crum helped a ninety-four-year-old man onto the train, none other than William Walton Swaney, the boy who had come to Fayetteville aboard the town's first passenger train, now grown to the twilight of his years, using a cane to climb the steps of the passenger car and embarking on his last ride aboard a Frisco passenger train. Swaney died three years later and is buried at Combs Cemetery.

Frisco continued its freight service until 1980, when it merged with Burlington Northern Railroad, which leased the line between Monette and Fort Smith to the newly formed Arkansas & Missouri Railroad in 1986. The A&M Railroad purchased the route in 2001 and continues to operate freight trains and an excursion train along the line.

Harnessing Mother Nature

In the evening of April 18, 1880, a tornado swept into Fayetteville along a line from Rochier Heights across the Fayetteville Square, down the Hollow and back up the western side of East Mountain (present-day Mount Sequoyah), where it caused significant damage and killed at least two people. It was one of several devastating tornados that hit northern Arkansas and southern Missouri the same evening.

The tornado crossed the Fayetteville Square and destroyed numerous buildings, including the three-story Tremont Hotel, where Victoria Glass was killed in the wreckage. Her husband, Hugh, the hotelkeeper, was severely injured but survived, as did their two daughters. The child of Rinda Mecklin was picked up on the west side of the Hollow and thrown across the area, dying from injuries. More than a dozen people were also injured.

The front of Thomas Boles's store on the southside of the square was ripped away from the rest of the building, spun upside down and backward and dropped into the same position leaning against the front of the rest of the building. The building that was home to the International Order of Odd Fellows, as well as nearly all other buildings on the south side of the square, was totally destroyed as well. Baum Brothers store on the west side was obliterated. "The track of the tornado was about 30 feet wide, and not a single building or fence in its course escaped destruction or injury. Barns, out-houses, fences and trees were all swept away."[94]

Dozens of homes were destroyed or severely damaged. Sam and Martha Young's house on East Mountain Street was also destroyed. Sam Young, a butcher who worked at a slaughterhouse on Huntsville Road, had no choice but to pick up surplus lumber and rebuild a new house. They reared two daughters and grandchildren in the house.

While some natural phenomena were impossible to control, Fayetteville set about controlling what it could. Major utilities began arriving in Fayetteville during the last decade of the nineteenth century. In 1886, the Fayetteville Telephone Company was started, but Bell Company patents kept the local company from proceeding until it purchased new equipment from Bell. William N. Gladson, professor of electrical engineering at the Arkansas Industrial University, took the lead, working with W.S. Bentey to build a switchboard on the third floor of the old Bank of Fayetteville Building at the northwest corner of the square.

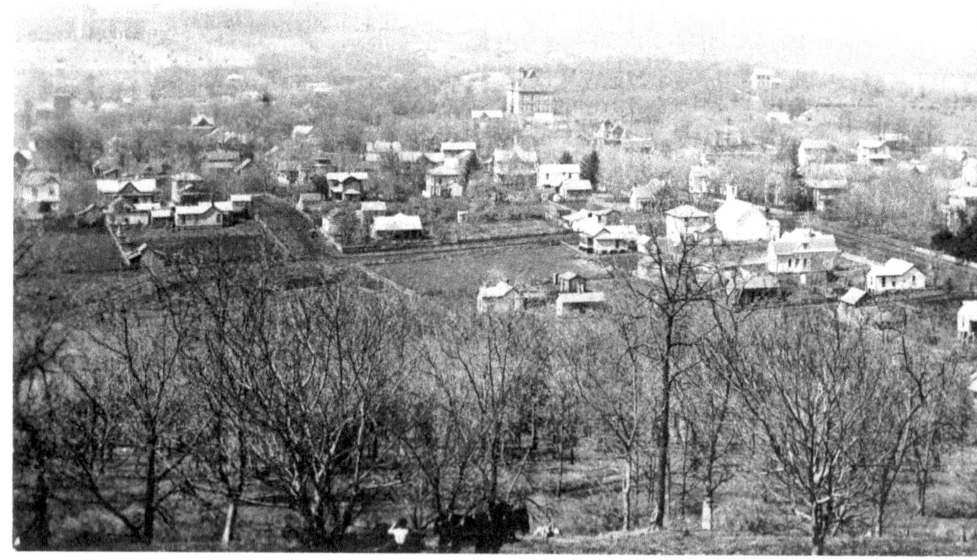

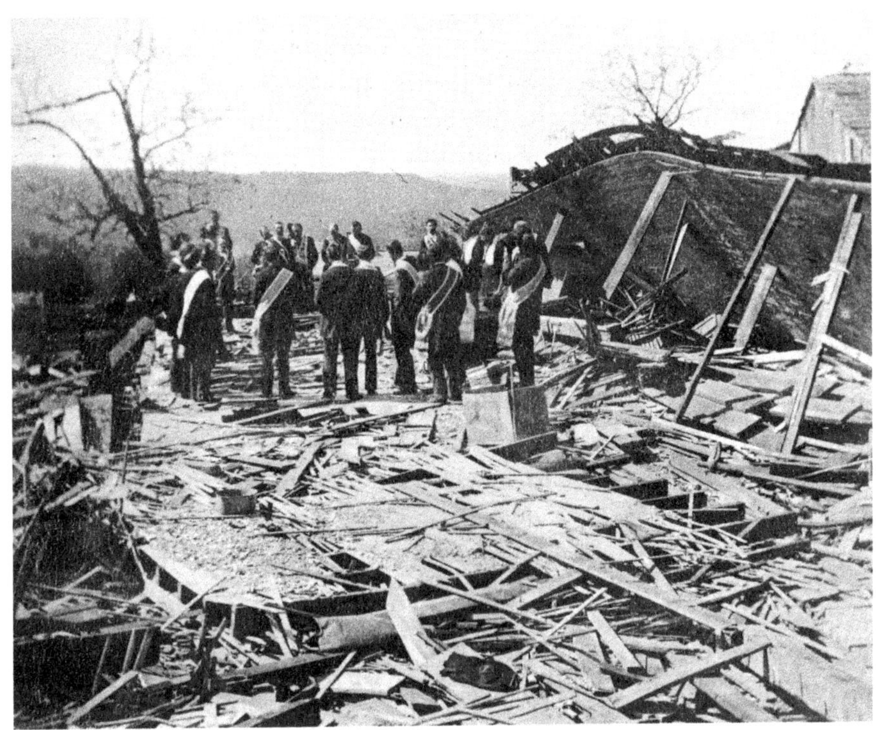

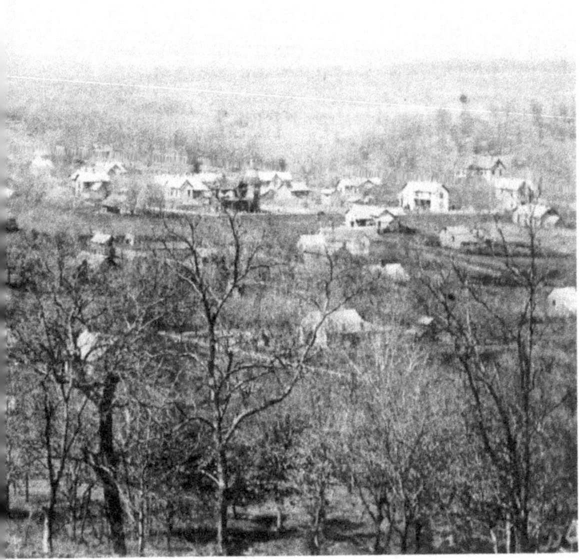

Above: Members of the International Order of Odd Fellows examine the remains of their hall following a tornado at Fayetteville on April 18, 1880. *Courtesy Shiloh Museum of Ozark History, Washington County Historical Society Collection, P-3157.*

Left: The Washington-Willow neighborhoods, known as the Masonic Addition when development began in the 1870s, are seen here in about 1890, with Mount Nord and the university campus in the distance. Today, the neighborhoods are part of the Washington-Willow Historic District. *Author's collection.*

Lola Ellis and Maggie Jackson were the first operators for the phone company. They worked a twelve-hour shift from 7:00 a.m. to 7:00 p.m. daily. Ellis continued working for the phone company into the 1950s. In the early days, Gladson began assigning two-digit numbers to people who subscribed to the telephone company. When a woman refused to take no. 13 as her phone number, Gladson took it as his own and assigned her no. 14.

Before 1888, Fayetteville's streetlight system consisted of four coal-oil lanterns mounted on posts at each corner of the square. Early efforts to provide "juice" from the Old Red Mill on the south side of Fayetteville and then the Roller Mill near the depot couldn't be sustained financially. Gladson, who had led the telephone installation, took the lead on Fayetteville's effort to establish an electrical plant in the city. He and James H. McIlroy purchased equipment in St. Louis and constructed a new plant at a spring near the western end of Spring Street, about where Powerhouse Seafood operates today.

A spring underneath the building provided water for a single boiler used to generate steam and run an electrical generating turbine. The crew consisted of a fireman to keep the boiler operating and an electrician. They would work what they called a daylight shift. When there was no daylight, they worked from sundown to sunup, and on cloudy days, they worked whenever electricity needed to be generated to power the city's electric lights. Carl Bennett recalled that after shutting down the plant in the morning, he would then spend the day wiring new homes or extending the mains on poles. He worked for about sixteen hours per day for sixty dollars per month in the late nineteenth century. He described the electrical situation in not the most reassuring way: It was a series type of system, and every additional light was added to the same circuit and increased the needed voltage. With that setup, the voltage got up to the level of two thousand volts flowing through homes closest to the generating end of the line.

Edward A. Vandeventer, who grew up in Fayetteville during the late 1870s and 1880s, recalled the period before electricity, telephones and running water: "A man who had a spring on his property was king. Others had to dig wells or depend on cisterns."[95] Indeed, maps of the city from 1885 show wells or cisterns in the backyards of every other home, business and boardinghouse.

In 1894, the city got its first water system. Before then, dozens of wells dotted the landscape of Fayetteville. But dozens of outhouses did, too, and

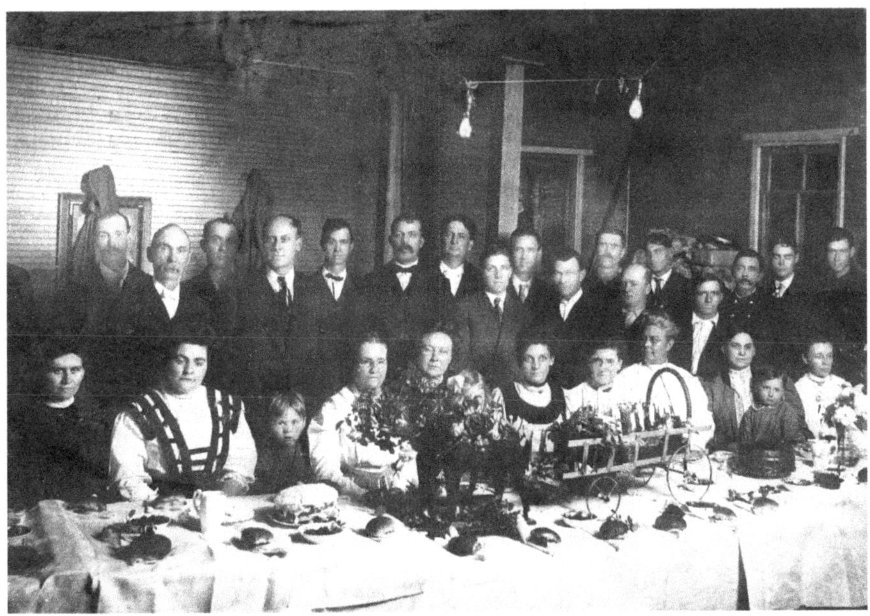

Members of the Fayetteville firemen's banquet, 1907. *Courtesy Shiloh Museum of Ozark History, Washington County Historical Society Collection, P-281.*

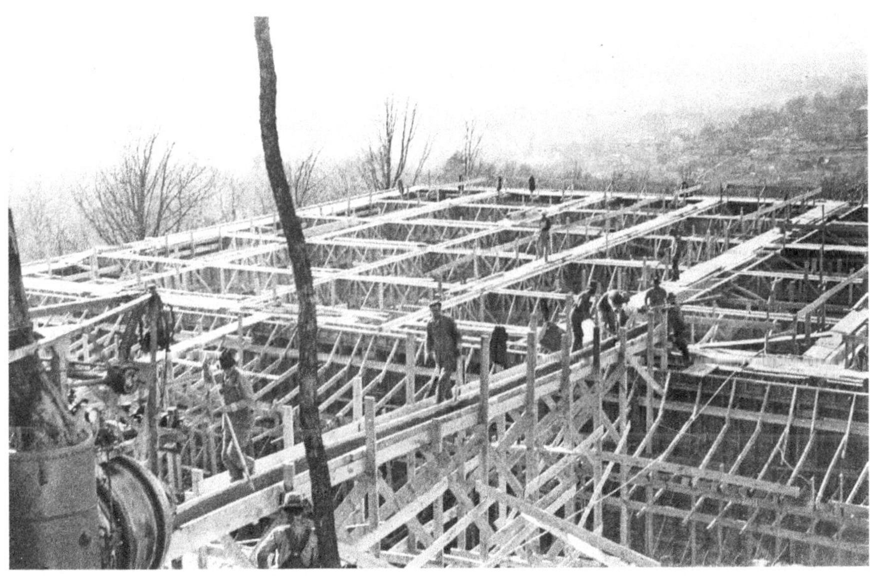

Workers pour concrete into forms to build a water-treatment plant on the southwest flank of Mount Sequoyah in January 1927. The city used the plant until the 1960s, when water began to be supplied by the Beaver Lake Water District. The treatment plant was razed in the early 2000s and turned into Mount Sequoyah Gardens Park. *Photo by Carl Smith. Courtesy Shiloh Museum of Ozark History, Ada Lee Smith Shook Collection, S-98-85-1397.*

the combination did nothing to improve health in the city. Brothers William B. and Charles A. Rees constructed a water plant on the West Fork of the White River at the eastern end of present-day Pump Station Road. The plant included a steam-powered pump to deliver water from the river valley to a reservoir on the west side of Mount Sequoyah, placed high enough to produce water pressure across the city.[96] Soon afterward, a volunteer fire brigade was organized.

Fayetteville Water Improvement District No. 1 was created in 1906, and the rickety wooden dam across the river that the brothers had built was replaced in 1907 with a concrete dam. A drought in 1909 dried up the West Fork for three months. Smaller dams were built upstream to impound emergency pools of water in case the main pool dropped again. This worked for a period, but the city eventually added a line from Clear Creek to increase water pressure. In 1927, a water treatment facility was added below the Mount Sequoyah water tanks.

In 1949, the city built Lake Fayetteville on Clear Creek to supply more water for the growing community. In 1958, the city acquired property on the White River to build Lake Sequoyah, again to supply more water. When Beaver Lake was built to supply water for the entire region, Fayetteville retired Lake Sequoyah and Lake Fayetteville as water supplies and razed the water treatment facility in the late 1990s, turning the hillside on which it stood into a park, Mount Sequoyah Gardens. Today, both the lakes are city parks with hiking trails, boat docks and educational and recreational facilities.

A Hot Old Time

In 1868, Washington County commissioned James Van Hoose and Thomas Pollard to oversee the building of a new courthouse, the fourth, at the center of the square. It was the first tangible evidence that law and order were being restored to the town and county.

Competing newspapers began publishing again. E.B. and W.B. Moore restarted their father's paper, the *Fayetteville Weekly Democrat*, while the *Fayetteville News* and the *Fayetteville Sentinel* joined the competition during the 1870s. The *Liberator* and the *Fayetteville Republican* provided even more competition, suggesting that Fayetteville's commerce had rebounded as well.

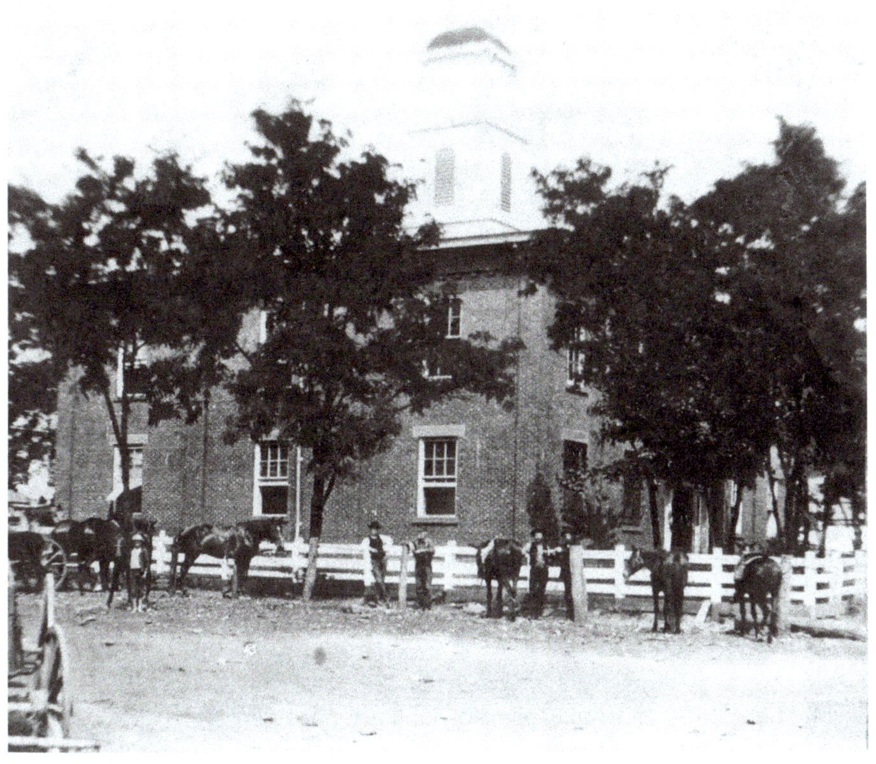

The county's fourth courthouse, pictured here in the 1880s, was built in 1870 after the third burned during the Civil War. A hitching line ran the perimeter of the courthouse grounds. *Courtesy UA Libraries, McIlroy Bank Collection, MC890.*

In the 1870s, however, as in many western towns and border regions, a lawlessness arose within Northwest Arkansas, spurred initially by the rise of a Republican government in Arkansas, which held power because those who had seceded were disenfranchised from voting or holding office immediately after the war. The disenfranchisement gave rise to groups such as the Ku Klux Klan and led to violence in Washington County, often aimed at law officers, newspaper editors and former Union supporters. In the late 1870s, one letter writer described a rough evening: "[T]here was a hot old time here last saturday. there was a lot of desperadoes in town and they had a fight and one fellow was shot. there was some 25 shots fired at one man. there was one fellow got down of his horse and stood behind it and fired 4 or 5 shot into the crowd, and they shot at him and shot his horse in the fore shoulder. I ges I have given you all the news."[97]

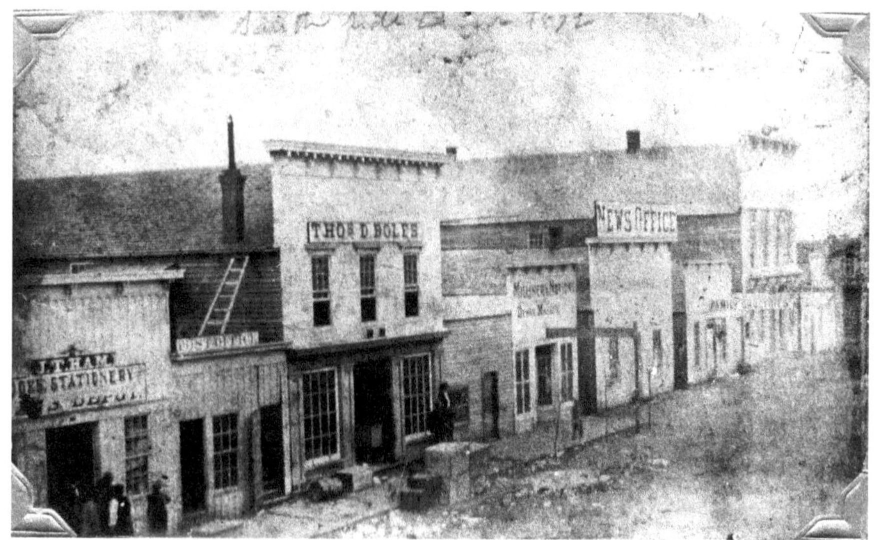

In 1872, the south side of the square, like all the other sides, was built mostly of wooden frame structures. J.T. Ham, who had served as county judge, sold books and stationery next door to the U.S. Post Office. Mrs. Lee and Mrs. Jennings operated a fashionable millinery and dress-making establishment mid-block. *Courtesy UA Libraries, William S. Campbell Collection, MC1427.*

The next spring, a similar night of violence occurred:

> *On the night of Sunday last, the Town of Fayetteville was entered by a mounted band of about 20 armed men. Several of them dismounted and proceeded on foot to the south-east corner of the public square, where both barrels of a shot-gun loaded with buckshot were discharged into a window of the Sentinel office. The party then moved deliberately by the residences of A.P. Farmer, Reuben Carter, and C.L. Summers, into all of which they fired shotted guns. The two parties joined near Summers's house, where they remounted and galloped off on the West Fork Road. There is no doubt the party was composed of men who, a week or more before, had threatened the town in revenge for the death of the ruffian, Reed, who was killed at the jail. The State Guards, after the pacific resolutions of the citizens meeting held by Reed's friends, had disbanded and the sudden attack in the dark found the city defenseless, and hence it was unchecked. Fortunately no one was hurt. After their departure a number of citizens armed and patrolled the town until daylight. The man Reed and the mob which created this disturbance are of a reckless class of people who have been the terror of law-abiding citizens since the early days of the war. Reed had killed several*

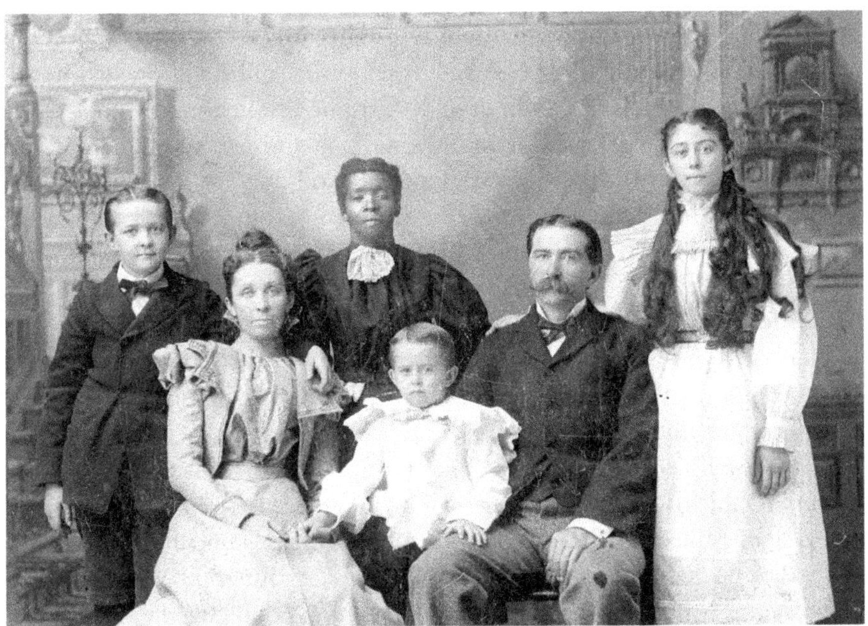

Adeline Blakely, born a slave in 1850, stayed with her family after the Civil War because "the Blakeleys were my people." The photo here dates to 1898. *Seated, from left to right*: Leonora "Nora" Izetta Blakeley Hudgins, Harvey Zeno Ross Hudgins and Harvey Masburn Hudgins. *Standing, from left to right*: Jay Guy Hudgins, Adeline Blakely and Elizabeth "Bess" May Hudgins. *Photograph by Sarah Jessie Young. Courtesy Shiloh Museum of Ozark History, Ann Wiggans Sugg Collection, S-2012-131.*

> *men, and had frequently ridden into town with his gang, harassing and annoying its inhabitants. A short time before his death he made such a foray into town, and while the Mayor was striving to maintain peace struck him on the head with a pistol. For this he was arrested and fined. Soon after this he was killed. Respectable people of his own party deny that politics had anything to do with the matter.*[98]

The threat of violence from the Reed Gang was such that state newspapers questioned whether students at the university would be safe in such a town. In 1881, the lawlessness reached its pitch. City Marshal W.S. Patton and Deputy Sheriff John Mount were killed on the square during a "reign of terror" involving the Reeds of West Fork.

Near the end of the century, a character of the Old West moved to Fayetteville from the nearby community of Goshen. His given name was Carl Ludwig von Berg. He immigrated to the United States in 1848, served in the Union army during the Civil War and became a U.S. scout out on the northern plains. By the time he came to Fayetteville, he still dressed in the style of the western scouts, with a wide-brimmed slouch hat, leather pants and jacket with fringe. With long, flowing hair and a ragged goatee, Von Berg could be easily mistaken for Buffalo Bill Cody, one of his fellow scouts. Von Berg organized the first Boy Scout troop in Fayetteville and opened his house as a museum to all who passed by. In 1908, Buffalo Bill's Wild West Show came to Fayetteville, and Von Berg was reunited with Cody and other friends from his scouting days.

Along with his apparel and unconventional look, Von Berg brought with him the culture of his frontier experience, telling tall tales about his exploits, some of which might have been true, and playing taps at sunset each evening. The bugle call was based on the "Scott Tattoo" and arranged by Brigadier General Daniel Butterfield during the Civil War as a more fitting final bugle call to signify the end of the day. Its solemn melancholy and association with the end of daylight led to it being played at military funerals. Von Berg lived high on the western flank of East Mountain, overlooking the city. When he played taps, all of the city could hear it. And when he died in 1918, Fayetteville residents swore they could still hear the clarion refrain of Von Berg's bugle, commemorating an end to his life and the frontier itself.

CHAPTER 5

A NEW CENTURY

As if to punctuate the importance of a new century, Fayetteville saw a surge in new construction at the beginning of the twentieth century. A U.S. Post Office was built at the center of the square. Many of the frame buildings still standing on the square were replaced with sturdy brick and stone structures. The Washington Hotel and the A.F. Wolf building, both three stories tall, were built on Mountain Street. City Hospital was erected on School Avenue. Congregations of the Baptist church, the First Presbyterian Church and Cumberland Presbyterian Church and the Catholic church all built new commodious churches. The Knights of Pythias erected a large opera house on College Avenue, a group of residents organized the Airdrome Theatre Orchestra and Frank Barr began showing silent pictures at his Lyric Movie House. The nicest homes in the city sprang to being on the brow of Mount Nord, including the Arkansas House, which was built for the St. Louis World's Fair, dismantled afterward, shipped to Fayetteville and rebuilt to become the city's closest thing to the Parthenon, a gleaming white building of Corinthian columns and broad entablatures beaming at the western crest of the mount. The county erected a new Washington County Courthouse at the intersection of College Avenue and Center Street in 1905.

One of the courtroom's early cases was notable for its defendant: Hugh A. Dinsmore, a former U.S. congressman from Fayetteville who also was appointed by President Grover Cleveland as America's second minister to Korea. He was accused of assault and battery with attempt to kill the

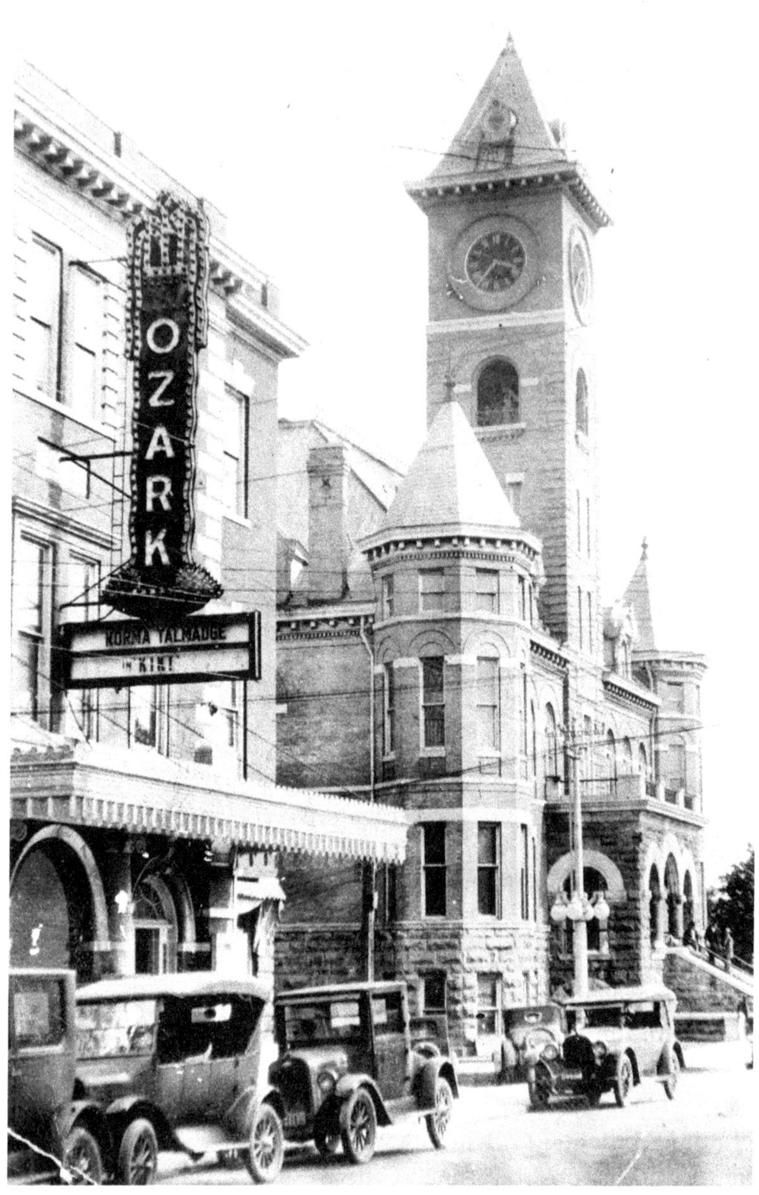

Near the beginning of the twentieth century, the county government approved erection of a new county courthouse at the intersection of College Avenue and Center Street. Next door to it, the Knights of Pythias built an opera house that soon became known as the Ozark Theatre, which offered theatrical performances, Chautauqua speakers, vaudeville acts and moving pictures. The theater operated until the mid-1970s and was converted to business offices. *Courtesy UA Libraries, William S. Campbell Collection, MC1427.*

governor of Arkansas, Jeff Davis. Dinsmore claimed that he confronted the governor at the Washington Hotel while the governor was in town campaigning for the U.S. Senate. Dinsmore believed the governor possessed a letter Dinsmore had received from Davis's rival, Senator James H. Berry, and that had been stolen from his desk. In trying to retrieve the letter, Dinsmore apparently hit Davis, who in turn struck Dinsmore with his cane, the same cane Davis had used to strike Carroll D. Wood, an assistant judge of the Arkansas Supreme Court. Dinsmore pulled out a revolver and pistol-whipped Davis.

At trial, Dinsmore testified that he had not tried to kill Davis but simply wanted possession of his letter. The governor did not appear at the trial, but a witness, described as a "drummer," testified that he had listened to Davis read the letter in question while traveling to Fayetteville by train. Dinsmore testified, "I struck the first blow. I would have struck the last blow if they hadn't prevented me from doing so. I would have struck other blows, also, and do not think Davis got what he deserved."[99] Dinsmore was fined one dollar for the assault and the minimum fine of fifty dollars for carrying a concealed weapon.

The early part of the century, though, was less about old grudges and more about new possibilities. In 1911, pilot Glenn Martin became the first person to fly an airplane in Fayetteville, taking off and landing at the Washington County Fairgrounds, which were then near the present-day corner of Razorback Road and Martin Luther King Jr. Boulevard. Martin was a pioneer aviator who went on to found an aircraft company that today is known as Lockheed-Martin. Another would-be innovator, Jerome S. Zerbe, designed what he called an "air sedan" that was intended to carry more people than the small biplanes were able. His creation had four cambered wings above a gondola-like compartment. Reports indicated that the pilot, Tom Flannery, did get the plane into the air for a short flight, but little is known what happened afterward to the plane or to Zerbe.

About a decade later, a young woman named Louise McPhetridge, who lived in Fayetteville while attending the University of Arkansas, made her own aviation news. In 1929, she won the Women's Air Derby, competing against pioneer aviators such as Pancho Barnes and Amelia Earhart in the transcontinental race. She and Earhart formed the Ninety-Nines, an international organization of female pilots that continues to this day. Then she won the Bendix Trophy Race against all comers, both male and female pilots. She set world records for speed, altitude and endurance, staying aloft more than eight days. She described some of the difficulties in the latter accomplishment beyond the normal issues of eating and sleeping while flying: "There were two hundred gallons of gasoline to pump every twenty-four hours by a hand pump which wobbled a half pint each full stroke. There was oil to pump, rocker arms to grease, batteries to change, an hourly log to keep. A hundred and one things."[100]

Consolidation of the School District

The number of students finishing their primary grades caused the Fayetteville School Board to pursue construction of a high school on School Avenue, opening in 1908. The original building cost $35,000, but north and south wings were added in 1925 and 1927 at a cost of more than $20,000 each. During the Depression, a federal project was approved for the high school. A gymnasium that had been on the University of Arkansas campus, known by university students as "Schmidt's Barn,"

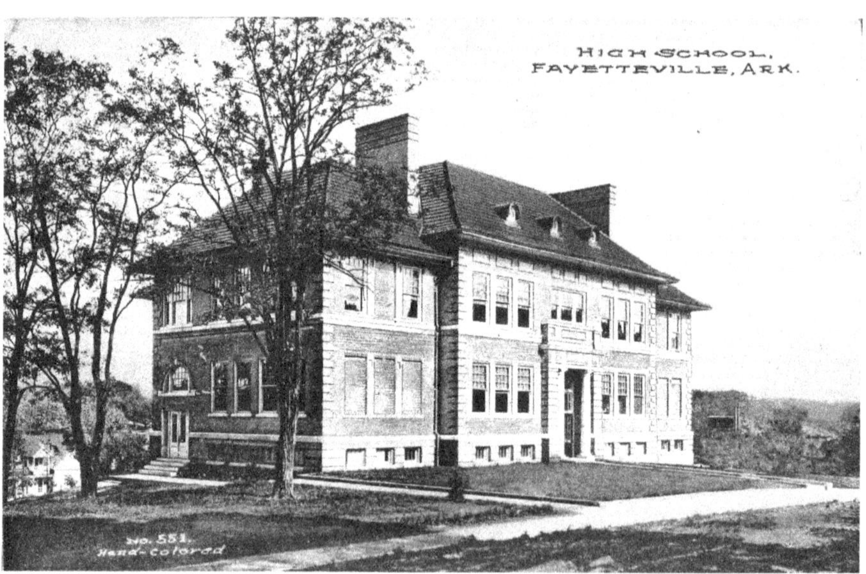

The first Fayetteville High School was built at the crest of School Avenue in 1908. The small wings on the left and right were extended in the 1920s as the school enrollment increased. In 1952, a new high school was built, and this building was converted into Hillcrest Junior High. After a fire in the late 1960s, the building was razed and is the site of Hillcrest Towers today. *Author's collection.*

was sold to the Fayetteville district and moved to the high school block, providing the steel framework, wood exterior and lighting system. The school district then erected a large stone entrance using rock quarried from South Mountain.[101]

Historian William Campbell noted the strong involvement of the Parent-Teacher Association in developing the early schools as well as individuals: "One of the outstanding personal contributions to the schools was the gift of Leopold E. Baum of $500 to the high school. He had no children, but wished to contribute a perpetual beneficience [*sic*] to the youth of Fayetteville."[102]

Along with these school buildings in town, small rural school districts were organized outside the Fayetteville district, with one-room schoolhouses being established in chapels or community buildings. By the early part of the twentieth century, though, these small schools began dissolving and merging with other nearby similar schools. The state also passed legislation in 1927 requiring districts that had fewer than fifteen pupils or that met less than six months to dissolve and made the limits even stricter two years later.[103]

For instance, the Grady School District 157, also referred to as Dowell's Chapel, and the Elm Grove District 149, known as Neally's Chapel, were relatively near each other at opposite ends of Cato Springs Road. In 1917, the memberships of both decided to join their schools together, quite literally, hauling the Grady School building east to the Elm Grove School, where they were attached one to the other. This new larger school was renamed Midland School and merged with the Fayetteville district. Midland, like so many of the rural schools, drew water from a well. Two "five-hole" privies were set at corners of the property.

One student, Edward Moran, recalled attending the school in 1918 and an instance in which some boys put a skunk in the heating stove:

> *We did not have school the next day since the scent of the skunk remained. It didn't take the teacher long to discover the culprits, and they were punished.... We had a large playground and we played all sorts of games. The boys played a lot of baseball, but there was not such thing as football....Just before Christmas we had pie suppers to raise money for presents for all the children in the neighborhood....There were about 65 children, at least, going to school when I went there....It is too bad that children nowadays can't go to a country school. Those memories are the most wonderful in the world for those of us who attended a country school.*[104]

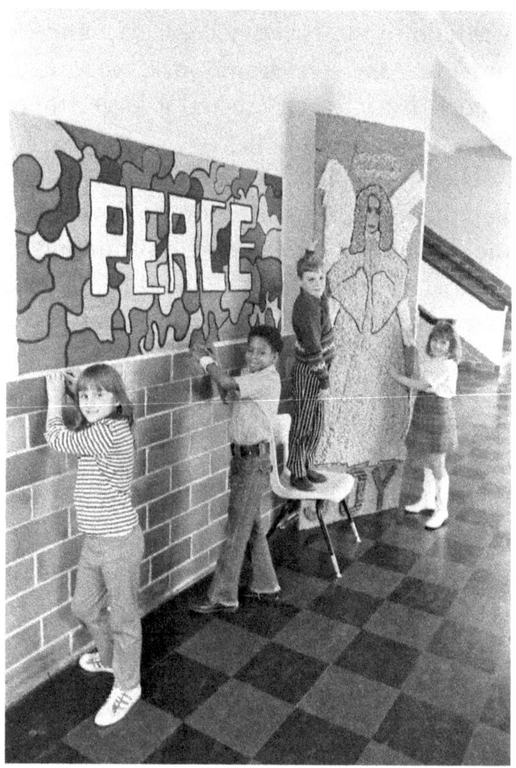

Four students—Thelma Plumlee, Tony Thompson, Roger Hall and Becky McClendon—decorate the halls of Jefferson Elementary School on December 12, 1972. *Photo by Ken Good. Courtesy* Northwest Arkansas Democrat-Gazette *and Shiloh Museum of Ozark History/*Northwest Arkansas Time *Collection, NWAT 12-21-1972.*

Midland closed in 1945. On one cold day, the stovepipe fell, covering the students, books and desks with soot. Virgil Blossom, who had been a principal at Midland but was by then an administrator, came out and tried to fix the pipe. The result was that his white shirt was turned black. Failing in this effort, the students were all transferred to Jefferson School at midterm.

In 1949, the state passed legislation that further curtailed the small schools and forced them into the larger school districts. Those coming into Fayetteville over the course of the first half of the century included Appleby, Baldwin, Braden, Buckner, Comb's Chapel, Goshen, Mayfield, Meadow Valley, Mount Comfort, part of Rieff's Chapel, Salem, Son's Chapel, Sycamore and Wyman.

During the 1950s, the school district began building elementary schools across the growing city. Bates Elementary opened in 1951, and Root Elementary was built in 1955, both using a design featuring Maximlight construction, patented by local architect T. Ewing Shelton.

Asbell Elementary opened in 1962 to accommodate a growing population on the northwest side of town. Butterfield Elementary opened in 1968 as the state's first open-space elementary school. The first Happy Hollow Elementary opened in 1972; the current Happy Hollow building replaced it in 2011. The school was the first in the district to follow a continuous learning calendar that uses a schedule with more frequent, shorter breaks instead of a long summer vacation.

Along with the new elementary schools, the school district also built a new high school on Stone Street, opening in 1952, and converted the old high school into the city's first junior high, Hillcrest Junior High.[105] Woodland Junior High was built in 1960, and Ramay Junior High opened in 1966 to replace the closing of Hillcrest Junior High.

A variety of private and parochial schools was organized as well, including St. Joseph's Catholic School, the Fayetteville Christian School, the New School and Haas Hall.

The school district added middle schools in 2000 to take care of grades five and six, allowing the crowded elementaries more room. McNair Middle School was built on Mission Boulevard on the east side of town, and Holt Middle School opened on Salem Road near the Mount Comfort community on the west side of town. Owl Creek School, which included both an elementary school and a middle school, was built in 2006 on the west side of Fayetteville to serve the quickly growing neighborhoods. Most recently, the district added "Virtual Academy" to provide online educational opportunities.

Jefferson Highway and U.S. 71

The modern-day driving route between St. Louis, Missouri, and northern Arkansas follows what was originally one of the primary Osage trails, generally sticking to the high ground separating the Missouri River watershed to the north from the White River watershed to the southeast. The subsequent Military Road, U.S. highways and St. Louis & San Francisco Railroad followed parallel paths to establish transportation into the region.

The way from Fayetteville south to Van Buren was less distinct, with the earliest route crossing the Illinois River, running southwesterly to Cane Hill and then turning south to run down the western edge of the state and into Van Buren on the Fayetteville Road. Another route

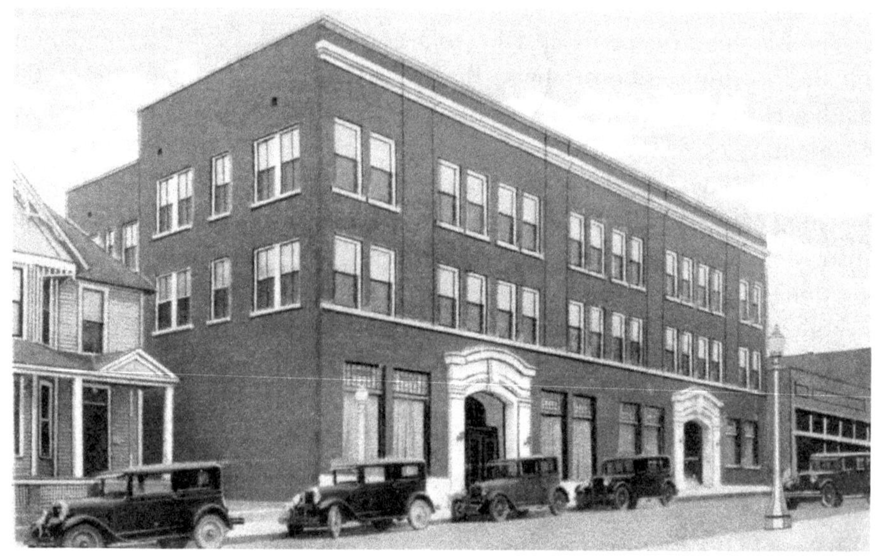

The Mountain Inn on Center Street grew from a boardinghouse originally known as the Mountain House into the largest hotel in Northwest Arkansas by the 1960s. It was sustained by the growing automotive traffic through Fayetteville during the twentieth century. *Author's collection.*

followed the valley of the West Fork of the White River, up over the Boston Mountains and down Frog Bayou to Alma. The Washington County Circuit Court appointed three commissioners in 1829—Larkin Newton, John Billingsley and Nathan Caughman—to mark a route from Fayetteville south to the county line. The route they marked ran south-southwest, splitting the difference between the two existing traces. It ran to Cove Creek and then stayed on the ridge east of Cove Creek. Today, most of the route is Arkansas Highway 265 south through Hogeye and Strickler, where it becomes the dirt road known today as Bug Scuffle Road, which has changed very little in the last 180 years. Overseers were appointed to take charge of various roads in the county to make sure they remained in good condition.

Soon, roads spread like the legs of a spider from Fayetteville toward all points of the compass and brought travelers from each point back toward Fayetteville: Carrollton Road leading northeasterly toward Carrollton and then southeasterly to Batesville; Huntsville Road leading due east to the county seat of Madison County in the heart of the Ozark Mountains; Ozark Road, now known as the Pig Trail, leading southeasterly to Cass and Ozark; West Fork Road leading south to West Fork and over the Boston

Mountains to Alma; Wedington Road heading west to the Indian Territory; Osage Springs Road leading north to Bentonville; Cane Hill Road leading southwesterly; and Cassville Road leading due north to Missouri.

The dirt roads that connected Fayetteville with Springdale during the mid-nineteenth century were thinly settled and little improved from the days of the Butterfield Overland Mail. One young traveler recalled his first wagon ride from Mud Creek north of town to the Fayetteville Square, passing only three houses in the late 1860s—the Appleby hewed-log house, the Robert Anderson place and the John Skelton farm. He passed several cabins owned by African American families at Red Hill and the Babb place near the present-day North Street. But then he didn't see another residence until reaching the Botefuhr and Mayes homes at the intersection of present-day Maple Street and College Avenue. The turn onto Center Street to get to the square presented a "long miry muddy street."[106] By the early twentieth century, they were little improved.

The rise of the automobile in the early 1900s, however, caused communities to form associations to improve these roads. Two proposals for grand north–

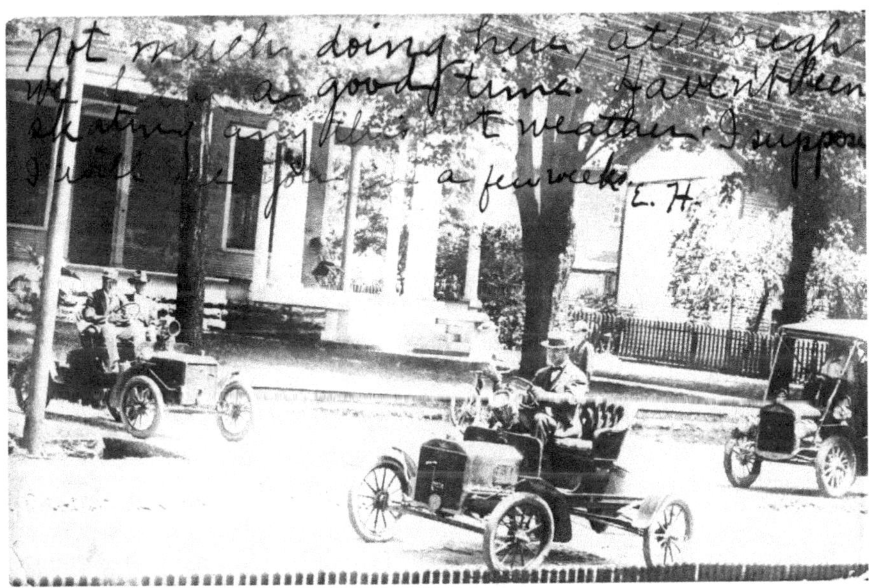

Several photo postcards were produced showing these drivers on Washington Avenue with what are believed to be the first automobiles in Fayetteville. Drivers included Harry Baum, Dr. Otey Miller and Dr. Charles Richardson. The sender of the postcard must have been inured to newfangled horseless carriages, writing, "Not much doing here." *Author's collection.*

south touring highways came to Fayetteville, one to be called the Jefferson Highway and a second to be called the Lakes-to-Gulf Highway.

The latter would connect Duluth, Minnesota, with Galveston, Texas. Although it drew some attention, the Jefferson Highway caught the imagination of Northwest Arkansas boosters.

In 1915, the Jefferson Highway Association formed to create the first north–south transcontinental highway in the United States running the height of the Louisiana Purchase. The association proposed to name the route in honor of President Thomas Jefferson, whose administration funded the Louisiana Purchase. The Jefferson Highway would run some two thousand miles from Winnipeg, Canada, to New Orleans, Louisiana, under the proposal. Communities and states along the potential route offered subscriptions in the hopes their town or county would end up part of the route, which colloquially was also referred to as the "Pines to Palms" highway. The subscriptions would help pay for route markers, grading of the roads and eventual paving.

Arthur Kepner, president of the State Bank of Gravette, was a leading proponent of Arkansas's involvement, arguing that the state should join forces with Missouri to keep the route from being run through Kansas and Oklahoma. When the first association meeting was held in New Orleans, though, only one representative from Arkansas attended, and by chance at that. Meanwhile, Oklahoma had forty-three delegates.

Undaunted, Arkansans in western Arkansas continued work to become part of the highway. The *Fayetteville Democrat* reported:

> *The Jefferson Highway will be one of the greatest roads in the country and Arkansas should not miss an opportunity to bring the route through the Ozarks from Joplin, Mo., on to Fort Smith and from there to Shreveport, La. It is estimated that this route would be 62 miles shorter than the proposed route though Oklahoma and we can secure it if we work. There will be a meeting of those interested in securing the road in Fort Smith early in February and we hope to have a large delegation there.*[107]

Boosters for the Jefferson Highway also cited the University of Arkansas among the reasons for Fayetteville's participation:

> *There have been only two objections made to Fayetteville as the location for the University. They were, unfiltered water and inaccessibility. We are about to remove them both.... We are having prepared plans to build*

> *good hard surface roads across the county, connecting up with the Jefferson Highway which will at the same time connect us up with good roads to all parts of the state. Then what will the Little Rock patriots...who covet the University stand on?*[108]

The legislators in Little Rock might have had other ideas. Instead of supporting the western highway, the state surveyed a diagonal route across Arkansas in 1917 and secured federal aid amounting to $332,000 to help pay for a highway from Seligman, Missouri, southeasterly through Eureka Springs, Harrison, Jasper, Russellville, Conway and Little Rock and then on to southeast Arkansas.[109]

The lack of state backing and the poor quality of western Arkansas roads caused the Jefferson Highway Association to choose a longer route through Oklahoma and Texas. The association's decision, however, left open the possibility that an Arkansas route could be added in the future.

By 1921, grading work was nearing completion between Fayetteville and Winslow. It would be two more years before the portion between Winslow and Van Buren would be finished. Ironically, the last section to be paved in Washington County occurred in 1924 between Fayetteville and Clear Creek: "Filling this gap gives a fine road from the Missouri line to Fort Smith and will relieve Washington County of the large amount of adverse advertising that this particularly bad piece of road caused."[110]

Filling the gap also meant that the highway could be added to the National Auto Trail system as part of the Jefferson Highway. The Fayetteville Good Roads Committee lobbied the Jefferson Highway Association to alter its route, which added the Arkansas highway to its system in 1928.[111]

When created, the route came from the south into Fayetteville along the Greenland Road (or School Avenue, as it became known in town). Over the years, the route used differing streets to connect with College Avenue: Center Street, Mountain Street and Dickson Street. Then it followed College Avenue north. In the early days, it became the Springdale Road.

The name of Jefferson Highway didn't last long because the U.S. National Highway System was inaugurated in 1926, and highways were soon given numbers instead of names. The Jefferson Highway through Arkansas became part of U.S. Route 71. The only remnant of the Jefferson Highway's name today is the similarly named Jefferson Bus Lines, which was founded in 1919 at the dawn of the motorcoach industry and provided transportation between cities up and down the Jefferson Highway. It

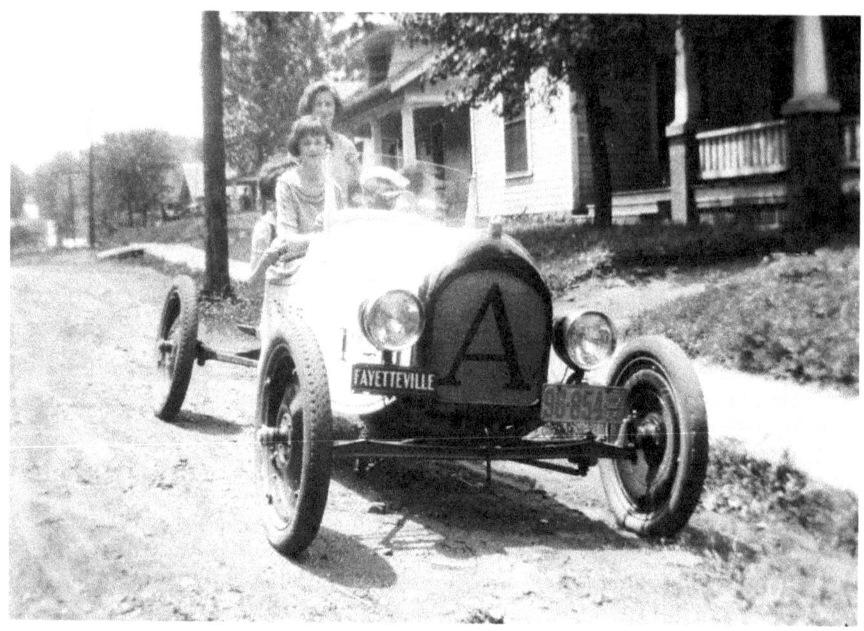

Most streets in Fayetteville were still dirt by 1924, when this photo of "Arkansas Traveler," a car built by Carl Smith, was made on Locust Street. *Photo by Carl Smith. Courtesy Shiloh Museum of Ozark History, Ada Lee Smith Shook Collection, S-98-85-1819.*

continues to serve Fayetteville, although its early bus terminal on College Avenue moved to South School Avenue in 1967 and then to a station just west of Interstate 49 on Wedington Drive in 2009.

At the beginning of the twentieth century, the portion of Route 71 that ran along College Avenue was justifiably referred to as one of the prettiest highways in America. Large maples, oaks and elms bordered the street and created an arching shady tunnel for motorists. Automobile traffic, however, contributed to the demise of the trees and residential nature of the highway. Service stations began opening along the avenue, then automobile dealerships, tourist motor courts and large groceries with even larger parking lots. A few homes, such as the Sonneman House, remain standing on College Avenue, but little evidence of the avenue's beauty remains.

In the 1930s, the federal government chose Fayetteville as the location for a Veterans Administration hospital to serve the medical needs of veterans from across Northwest Arkansas. Fayetteville was chosen in part because of its easy highway access, as well as its location on the railway line.

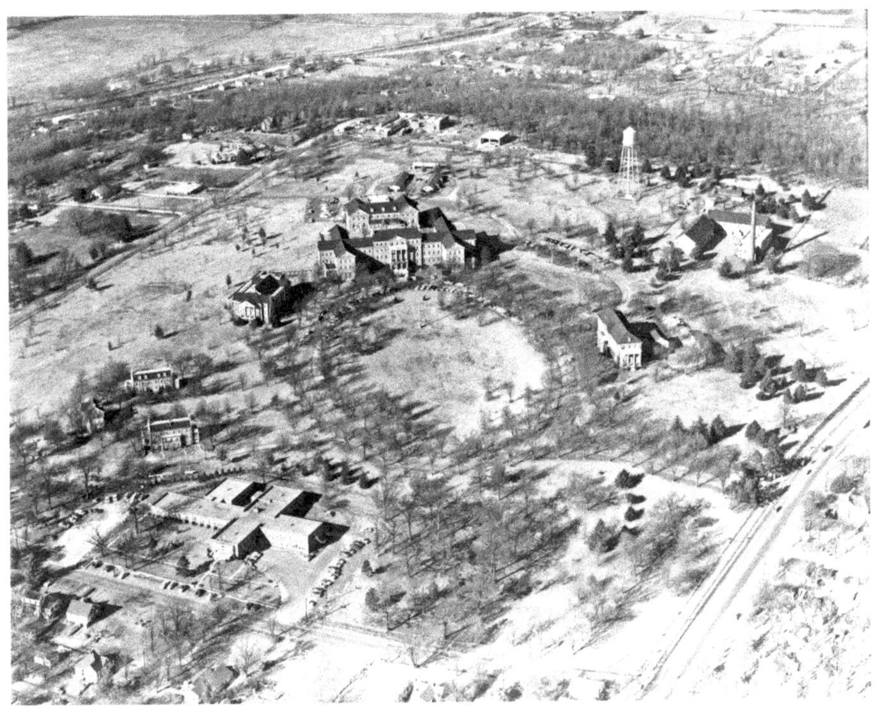

Built in 1934 atop Watermelon Hill, the Veterans Administration Hospital proved to be one of several federal projects that helped sustain Fayetteville's economy during the Depression. Pictured here in about 1959 (with Washington County Hospital in the lower left), the Veterans Affairs Hospital continues to serve the healthcare needs of veterans from across the region. *Courtesy Veterans Affairs Hospital.*

In 1952, the city built a wending connection for U.S. 71 that connected North College Avenue and South School Avenue without motor vehicles having to pass through the busy square. The new serpentine route, informally referred to as the "south bypass," was named Archibald Yell Boulevard following a campaign by the Washington County Historical Society to honor Fayetteville's "most illustrious citizen."[112]

Methodist Assembly and Mount Sequoyah

In the early 1920s, the Methodist Episcopal Church, South, began looking for a site that would allow members of its five-state conference to meet during a summer retreat and provide year-round opportunities for other gatherings. The City of Fayetteville offered $35,000, utility connections, construction of an all-weather road and four hundred acres across the top and eastern side of what was then known as East Mountain. When the Methodist commissioners accepted Fayetteville's offer, bells were rung across the city.[113]

East Mountain was renamed Mount Sequoyah in honor of Ssiquoya, the inventor of the Cherokee syllabary, the first written form of a Native American language. Ssiquoya, whose name is usually spelled in English as Sequoyah and who was also known as George Gist or George Guess, completed his syllabary in 1821. He moved to Arkansas in 1824, initially living near the Dwight Mission in Pope County and then setting up a blacksmith shop and salt works on Lee Creek.

The Methodists erected numerous buildings atop Mount Sequoyah—summer cottages, a cafeteria, the Epworth Lodge and the Elza-Stephens-Remmel Hall among others. Reverend Sam Yancey oversaw the operations as superintendent from 1927 to 1950. A cross was erected on the southwest corner of the campus at the edge of the mountain top, where it could be seen from across most of Fayetteville. The pullout at the cross became a favorite late evening destination for young adults who were out on a date and looking for an excuse to prolong their time together.

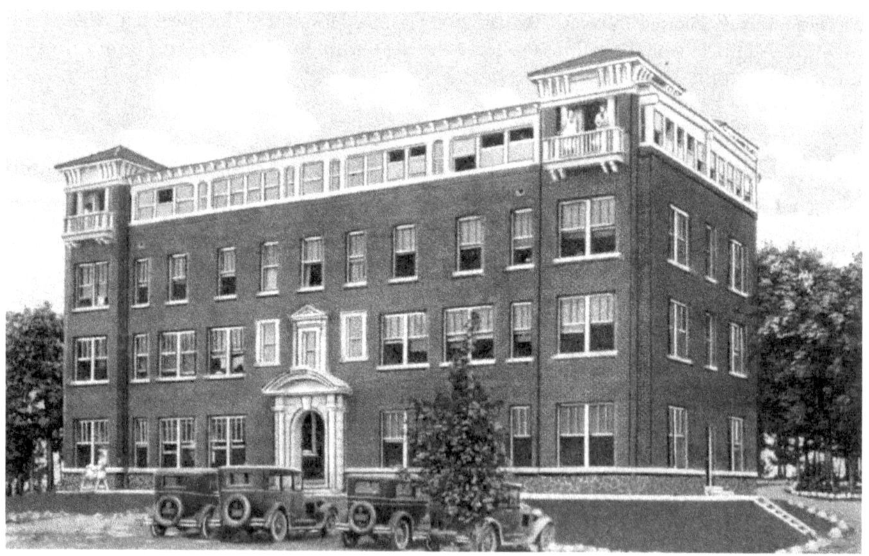

Remmel Hall, one of several buildings erected on the grounds of Mount Sequoyah Methodist Assembly, provided lodging for travelers attending Methodist enclaves on the grounds, as well as tourists who were passing through. *Author's collection.*

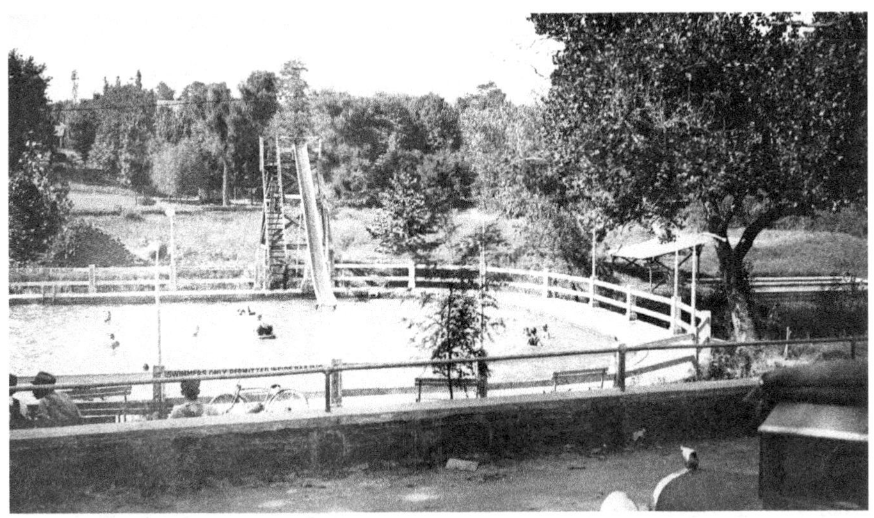

In the 1920s, the City of Fayetteville built a public swimming pool at Wilson Park, pictured here in about 1930, to replace Trent's Pond. *Photo by Carl Smith. Courtesy Shiloh Museum of Ozark History, Ada Lee Smith Shook Collection, S-98-85-1078.*

Mount Sequoyah continues to be used as a retreat center, although the United Methodist Church turned it over to a nonprofit organization in 2016. Fayetteville reacquired seventy-six acres of woods on the eastern side of Mount Sequoyah, added another thirty acres of donated land and created a park, Mount Sequoyah Woods, with hiking trails and a pavilion.

Although the Methodist Assembly provided a place for travelers to stay, the city developed its own travel park with a small motor court at Wilson Park. The city also drained Trent's Pond, a popular swimming hole, and built a new concrete swimming pool.

SURVIVING THE DEPRESSION

At the end of the 1920s, the booming economy also came to an end. The Wall Street crash of 1929 brought the nation to its financial knees. By the time Franklin Delano Roosevelt was inaugurated on March 4, 1933, the economy was in tatters and runs on banks had begun across the nation. By 1932, more than two hundred banks had failed in Arkansas. On the morning of Roosevelt's inauguration, Marion Wasson, the Arkansas bank commissioner, ordered all banks closed in the state and ordered them

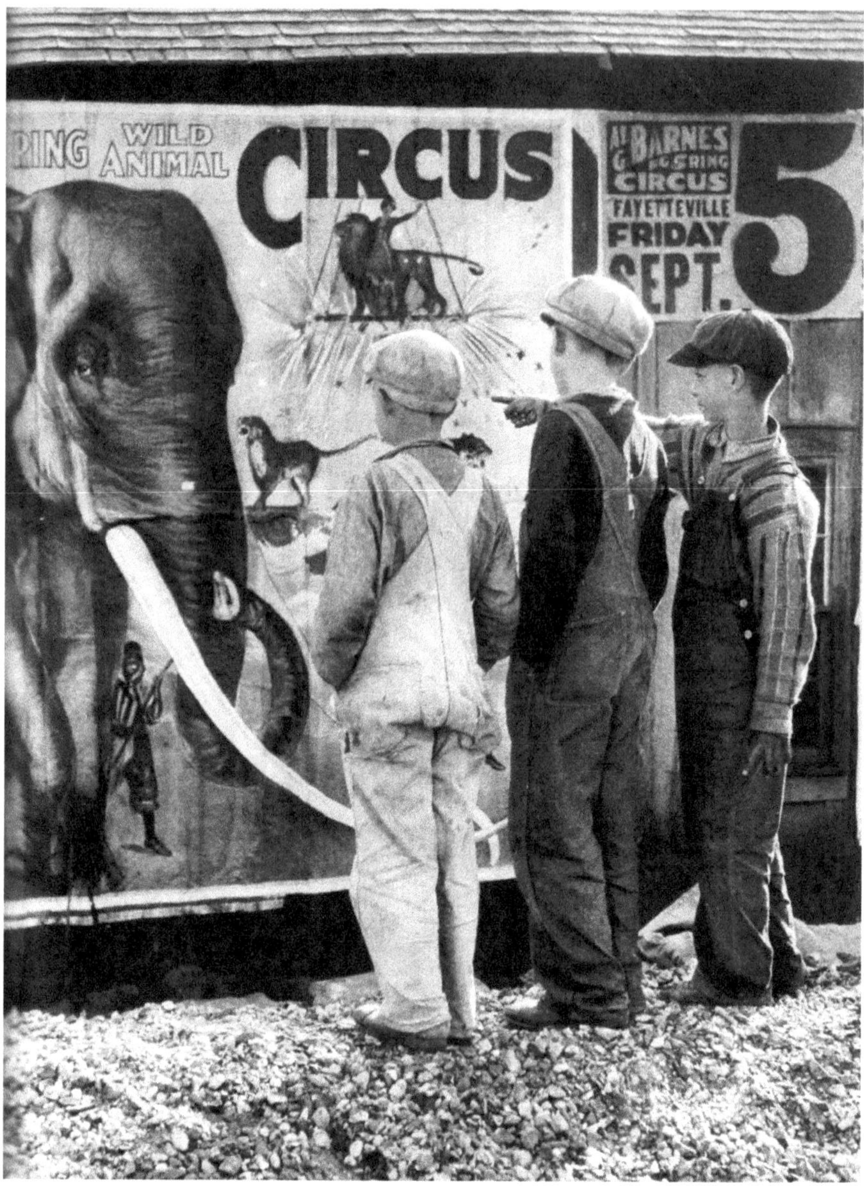

Boys examine the broadside posters announcing the coming of the Al G. Barnes Five-Ring Circus, which performed at the fairgrounds during the early 1930s. Many of the touring circuses eventually closed during the Depression era. *Photo by Julian Herman Fields.*

to remain closed until March 7. Roosevelt superseded the state order by proclaiming a national "bank holiday" and called for an emergency session of Congress.

Officials of the local banks issued a joint statement: "We have every reason to believe and assurance that the plans submitted will clarify the present situation and no doubt remove restrictions which will cause banks to operate on a more liberal basis."[114]

By that time, there were two banks in Fayetteville, First National Bank and Citizens Bank, and one savings and loan, the Fayetteville Building and Loan. First National Bank had acquired the smaller Arkansas National Bank in 1930 and First Savings Bank in 1932, perhaps preventing outright failure by either. At their peak before the crash, the banks and savings and loan had combined assets of nearly $5.6 million. By 1934, their combined assets had fallen to less than $3.9 million, a drop of more than 30 percent. Despite the drop in assets, the financial institutions in Fayetteville staved off failure. Over the next six years, they slowly regained their footing, finally reaching parity with their pre-crash levels in 1941.[115]

The policies and programs that Roosevelt's administration pursued were an aid to Fayetteville, as they were to much of the nation. Along with banking relief, the federal government started several agencies designed to put people back to work, including the National Recovery Administration, the Home Owners Loan Corporation, the Civil Works Administration, the Works Progress Administration and the Agricultural Adjustment Administration.

The National Recovery Administration had perhaps the most wide-ranging mission, licensing various sectors of the business community into "code authorities" with the power to determine production, pricing and pay within each sector. In Fayetteville, code authorities were created for retail grocers, wholesale grocers, hotels and restaurants, canneries, bakers, druggists, laundry cleaners, lumber yards, graphic artists, beauticians, painters, paperhangers and truckers, among others.

In some Fayetteville sectors, the codes proved useful. In others, they suffered from any ability to enforce the authority's decisions on recalcitrant members. Protests sprang up against the taxi services and laundry services, for instance, because these two sectors were charging prices above the NRA code prices. In 1934, Montgomery Ward withdrew its Fayetteville store along with the rest of its stores from the NRA without suffering any backlash. The canning companies, likewise, were getting good prices for products but didn't pass the profits on to the fruit and vegetable growers, paying them less than the price established by the NRA code.

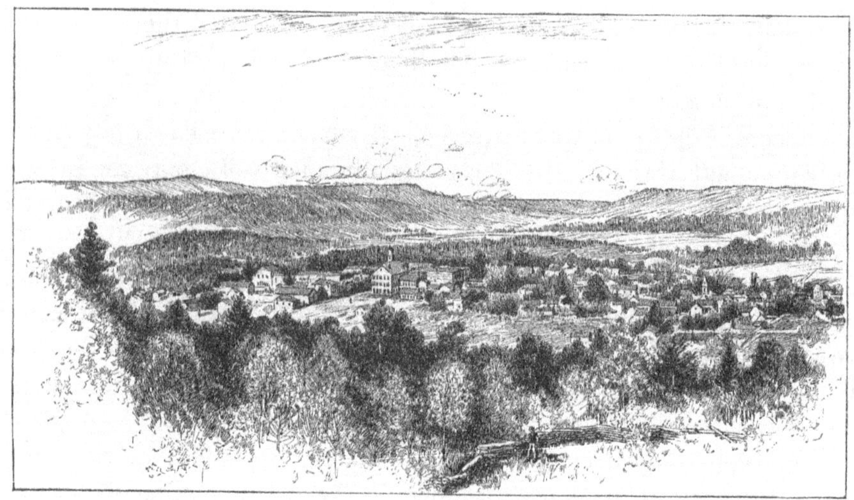

FAYETTEVILLE, ARKANSAS. FROM A PHOTOGRAPH.

A lithograph based on an 1870 photograph depicts Fayetteville not long after a new courthouse was built at the center of the square and the new three-story Winkleman Hotel, the largest frame building in the state at the time, was erected on Center Street. *Author's collection.*

Regardless, Fayetteville's economy bounced back more strongly than most towns in Arkansas and even at a pace that stood it well against the national recovery. In 1934, the Fayetteville Piggly Wiggly grocery store posted the sixty-third-best sales increase among 2,500 Piggly Wiggly stores across the nation. Even more so, the J.C. Penney store in Fayetteville recorded a bigger sales gain in 1934 than any other J.C. Penney store in the state and the third-largest gain among the chain's stores across the nation.[116]

The increase in commerce and confidence was noted by Roy Wood, chair of the local retail trades' code authority: "While it is too early to correctly evaluate NRA operations, any businessman anywhere, whether pro or into [*sic*] NRA, will have to admit that his sales have increased since August, that there is more money circulating, customers are buying easier and there is confidence in the future."[117]

One week later, C.H. Garrison of the Frisco Railway echoed Woods's remarks: "Fayetteville is one of Frisco's bright shipping points and also one of the bright spots of the whole country, both in receiving and sending freight."[118]

It was not all roses, though. The number of retail establishments dropped a little more than 10 percent between 1933 and 1935. Still, in weighing

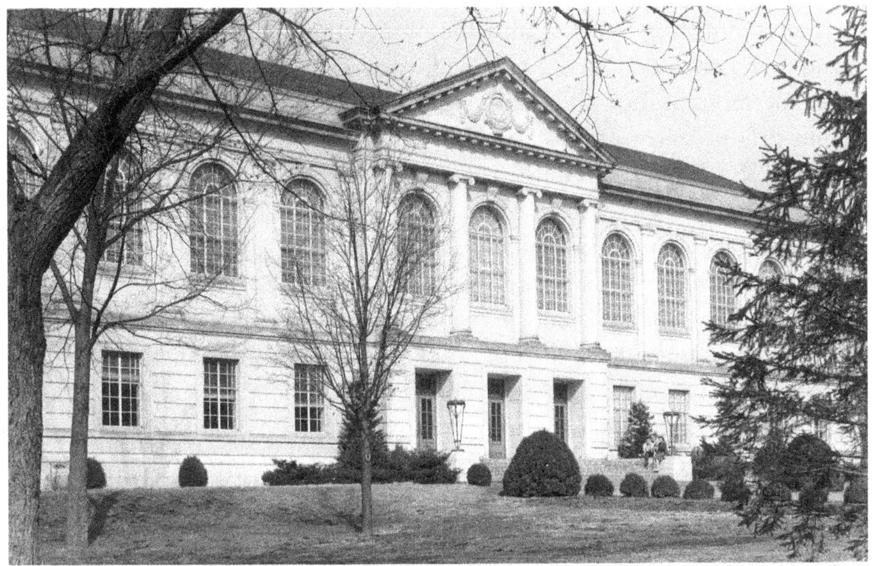

Vol Walker Hall was built in 1935 on the University of Arkansas campus, one of several campus buildings funded in part by federal recovery programs such as the Public Works Administration. The building served as the university's library for more than thirty years and is home now to the Fay Jones School of Architecture and Design. *Courtesy UA Libraries, William S. Campbell Collection, MC1427.*

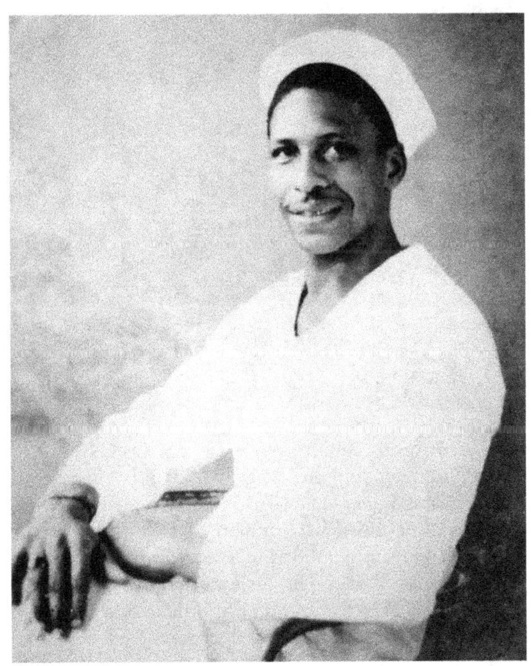

Sherman Morgan in his navy uniform is pictured in Honolulu, Hawaii, in 1943. Morgan served during World War II and then returned to Fayetteville, where he opened a popular café and billiard room on Rock Street. *Courtesy Shiloh Museum of Ozark History, Louis Bryant Collection, S-2001-49-5.*

the increase in total sales against the reduced number of retail shops, one researcher concluded that Fayetteville was experiencing a mild recovery and that most, if not all, local stores were profiting from the Roosevelt administration's economic policies.[119]

The U.S. Supreme Court ruled the federal legislation establishing National Recovery Administration an overreach by Congress, giving the executive branch more power than the U.S. Constitution allowed. By then, however, other federal programs had been approved to provide jobs, many aimed at public works projects. The university was a prime recipient of those projects, receiving federal help to build a new chemistry building, a library, a men's residence hall, an athletic field house and football stadium, a home economics building, a classroom building and a student union.[120]

In 1943, the city built a large hangar for airplanes at Drake Field. The "White Hangar," as it became known, was initially intended to provide a

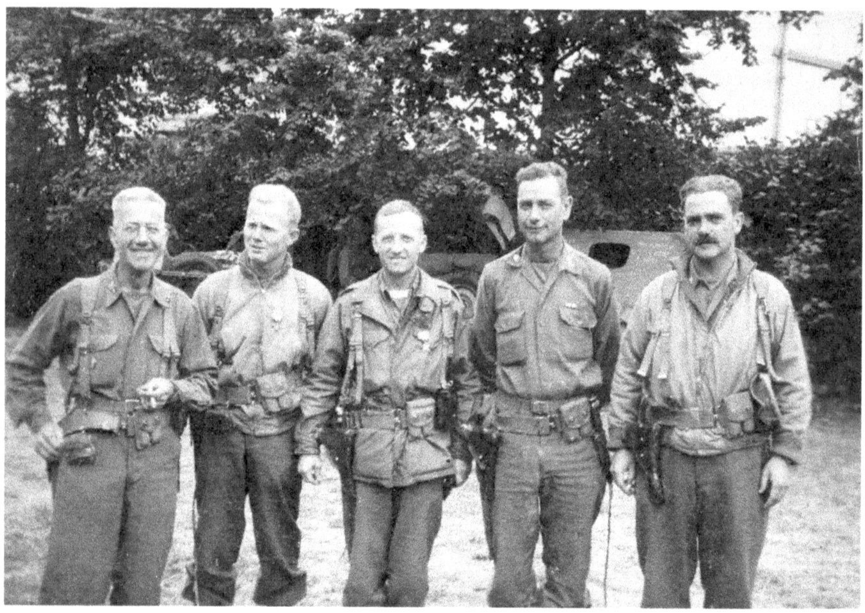

U.S. Army personnel, Europe, in about 1944. *From left to right*: Colonel Robert Bacon, Lieutenant Colonel Leroy "Fireball" Pond of Fayetteville, Lieutenant Colonel J.F. Smith, Lieutenant Colonel D.G. Gorton and Major Leonard Dull. Pond and Smith wear Silver Star medals. Pond was a graduate of Fayetteville High School and the University of Arkansas. He was wounded in action during late 1944 and evacuated to England, where he died a month later. He was awarded the Distinguished Service Cross with oak leaf cluster (twice), the Silver Star, the Bronze Star (twice), the Purple Heart (twice) and the French Croix de Guerre with silver star. *Courtesy Shiloh Museum of Ozark History, Gertrude Pond Collection, S-95-42-43.*

home for the University of Arkansas College Training Detachment during World War II. Wartime shortages of metal forced Fayetteville officials to think of a way to build a hangar using only wood. Henry George, an assistant city engineer, came up with the arched design. The building later served as headquarters for Scheduled Skyways, the city's first commercial airline, and is now home to the Arkansas Air and Military Museum.

Thoughts of the Depression ended as World War II began. Young men from across Fayetteville and the University of Arkansas campus enlisted to serve during the war. Leroy Pond served in the army in the European theater, while Sherman Morgan served in the navy in the Pacific theater. After returning home, Morgan opened a popular café and billiard hall on Rock Street, known simply as Sherman's.

CHAPTER 6
MODERN FAYETTEVILLE

After World War II, many of the nation's social conventions changed. Fayetteville proved to be one of the leaders in changing race relations. The town was perhaps ideally suited for dealing with the race issue at an earlier point than most of the South. While Arkansas was well within the Old South, Fayetteville was in the upper South and felt the cultural influences of the Midwest and Plains states. The population of African Americans in Fayetteville was fairly small, especially compared to many cities across southern Arkansas.

In 1948, Silas Herbert Hunt, a decorated veteran of World War II and graduate of Arkansas AM&N College, applied for admission to the School of Law at the University of Arkansas, which had not enrolled an African American student since its first year of operation during the Reconstruction period. Robert A. Leflar, dean of the law school, had already weighed the likelihood that a student of African American heritage would try to enroll and consulted the university's administration and board of trustees. His own opinion was that the university would be sued if it prevented a student from enrolling, and the university would lose the legal case. When Hunt walked into the registrar's office, Leflar was ready to enroll him. Hunt became the first student to break the color barrier at a traditionally white southern university.

Another student, Wiley Branton, came with Hunt and tried to enroll in the undergraduate program, but the university rebuffed Branton, arguing that Arkansas AM&N already provided undergraduate programs for African Americans.

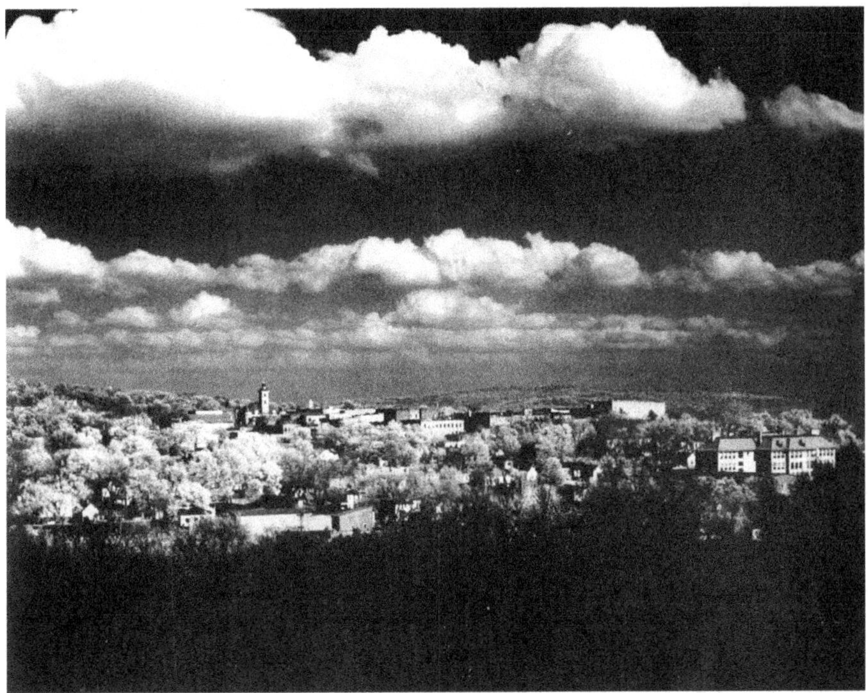

A view of downtown Fayetteville in 1951 shows the Washington County Courthouse on the horizon, the downtown area and old Fayetteville High School at the right. *Courtesy Arkansas Razorback.*

Hunt, who died of illness before he could finish his law degree, was awarded a law degree posthumously in 2008, and the building that houses admissions and enrollment services was named in honor of him in 1993. Nevertheless, he had started a process that could not be turned back. One month later, Edith Irby enrolled in the university's College of Medicine at Little Rock. Within a few years, the university began accepting African American undergraduates. Other issues fell one by one over time, as African American students protested for equitable housing on campus, hiring of African American faculty members and integration of athletic sports, each of which occurred over the next two decades.

The last major battle came in 1969 as the university prepared for what was being billed as the football game of the century, Arkansas versus Texas. President Richard M. Nixon and a bevy of politicians were planning to attend the game, and an organization of African American students on campus called for the Razorback Marching Band to quit playing "Dixie" during the university's pep rallies and games. The band and the student

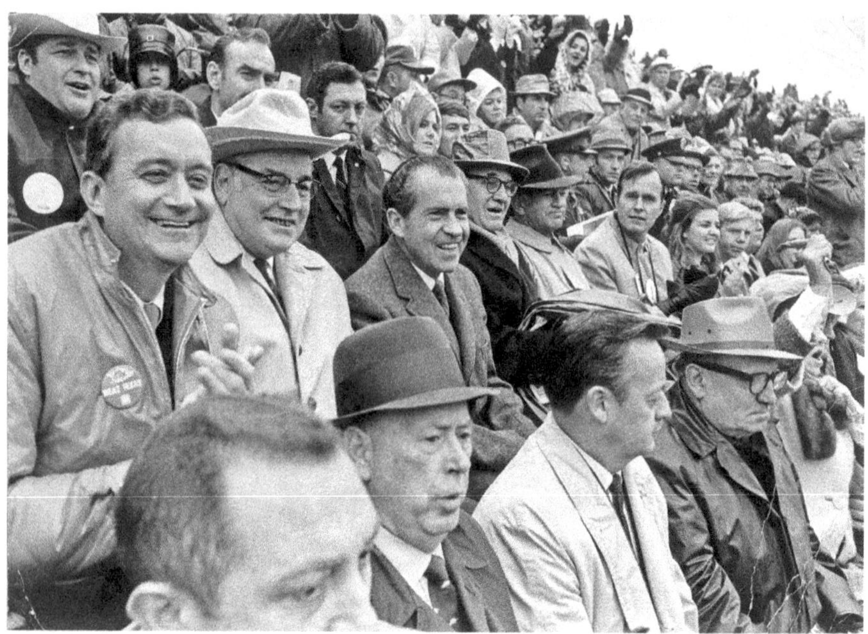

Razorback football games have always brought all manner of Arkansans together, but in 1969, the so-called game of the century between the University of Arkansas and the University of Texas brought a bipartisan group of politicians to Fayetteville. *From left to right*: U.S. Representative John Paul Hammerschmidt, Governor Winthrop Rockefeller, President Richard Nixon, Senators John McLellan and J. William Fulbright and U.S. Representative George H.W. Bush. *Courtesy UA Libraries, PC_OV-1-55.*

government voted to remove "Dixie" from the band's repertoire during the week leading up to the game.

At the local level, the schools of Fayetteville remained segregated from first grade through the eighth by 1954. But the school district had never created a high school for African American students, instead paying the cost of their education to attend one of the African American high schools in Fort Smith or Hot Springs. The African American community was small enough that this amounted to perhaps a dozen students attending high school away from Fayetteville. Some families made the choice to send their children to high school by boarding them at a home in Fort Smith, Hot Springs or even St. Louis, but many chose not to send their children away. Arkansas did not require students to attend school beyond the eighth grade at that time, so many students—black and white—ended their education after the eighth grade.

The Fayetteville School Board voted to integrate the high school just two days after the 1954 U.S. Supreme Court ruled in *Brown v. Board of Education* that separate educational facilities were unequal. Fayetteville and the Charleston school district near Fort Smith were the first in the old South to integrate. Among the reasons cited for integration was the savings that would accrue for not sending African American students to high school elsewhere. It's difficult to discern whether the board's stated rationale was simply a cover for the politically charged decision or if the financial concern was truly a primary cause.

Fayetteville made the decision to integrate the high school first and then add junior high grades and eventually elementary schools. Because of its size, Fayetteville received heavier newspaper scrutiny, including national stories distributed by the Associated Press. The relative smoothness of the high school integration, though, meant that the story quickly fell off the front pages. Seven African American students—two juniors and five sophomores—started at school in the fall of 1954. One person protested outside the high school. Inside the school, the European American students were prepped ahead of opening day to offer help to the African American students. By 1965, all the schools were integrated, and Lincoln School was closed.

Although integration had gone well on an institutional level, at a personal level, most of the African American students encountered some amount of animosity or outright hostility. Some students perceived some activities as being closed to African American students, while others activities were in

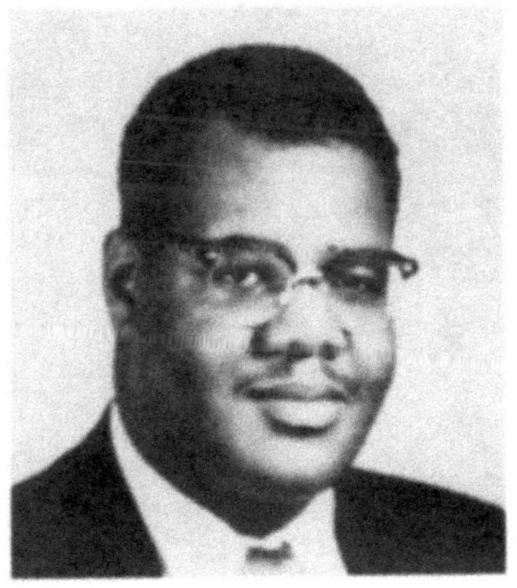

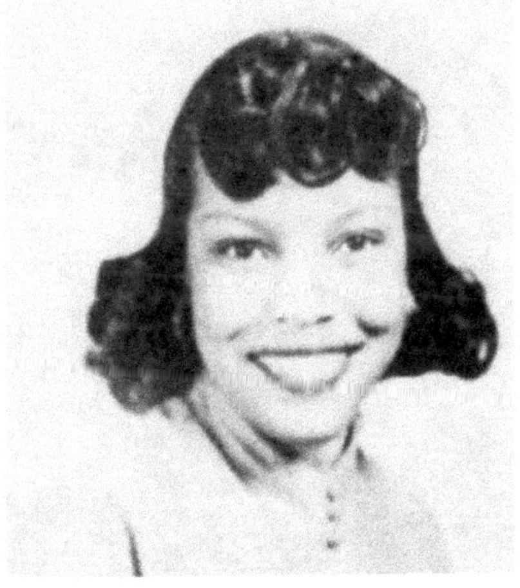

Preston Lackey and Peggy Ann Taylor were the first two African American students to integrate Fayetteville High School. *Courtesy Fayetteville School District.*

fact limited: African American students could join the high school band, for instance, but couldn't travel to performances. In other instances, racially motivated decisions by other districts affected Fayetteville's students. Several other school districts refused to play football with Fayetteville because the high school team was integrated.

A survey of African American students in 1962 was disconcerting. Only four of the eleven students interviewed offered positive written comments about school, and three of those were qualified. In discussion, the surveyed students generally felt that they didn't have equal opportunities for participation. One student said that "some of the teachers give higher grades to whites than to Negroes" when they do the same work. Likewise, students objected to the "expression and language of teachers," particularly one who used a racial slur in class and told "Negro stories."[121]

In early 1962, the Central Methodist Church appointed a Commission on Christian Social Concerns, which took up the question of how young African American residents of the city perceived their economic and social outlook. The commissioners asked students what their intentions were with regard to education after high school and eventual employment.

The commission's survey painted a bleak picture. Of the twenty young people interviewed, about half of them were in senior high school and

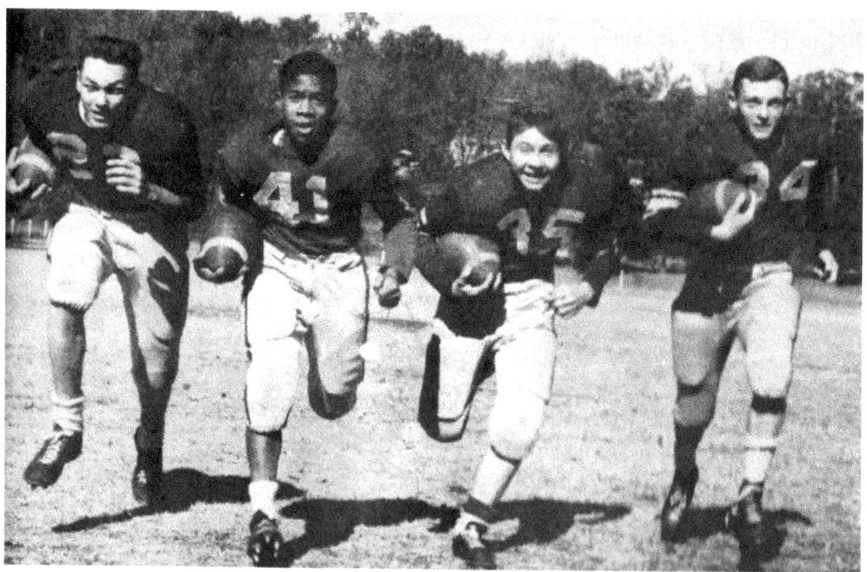

When Joe Manuel, *second from left*, and other African American students joined the Fayetteville High School football team, several competing schools forfeited their games rather than play against an integrated team. *Courtesy Fayetteville School District.*

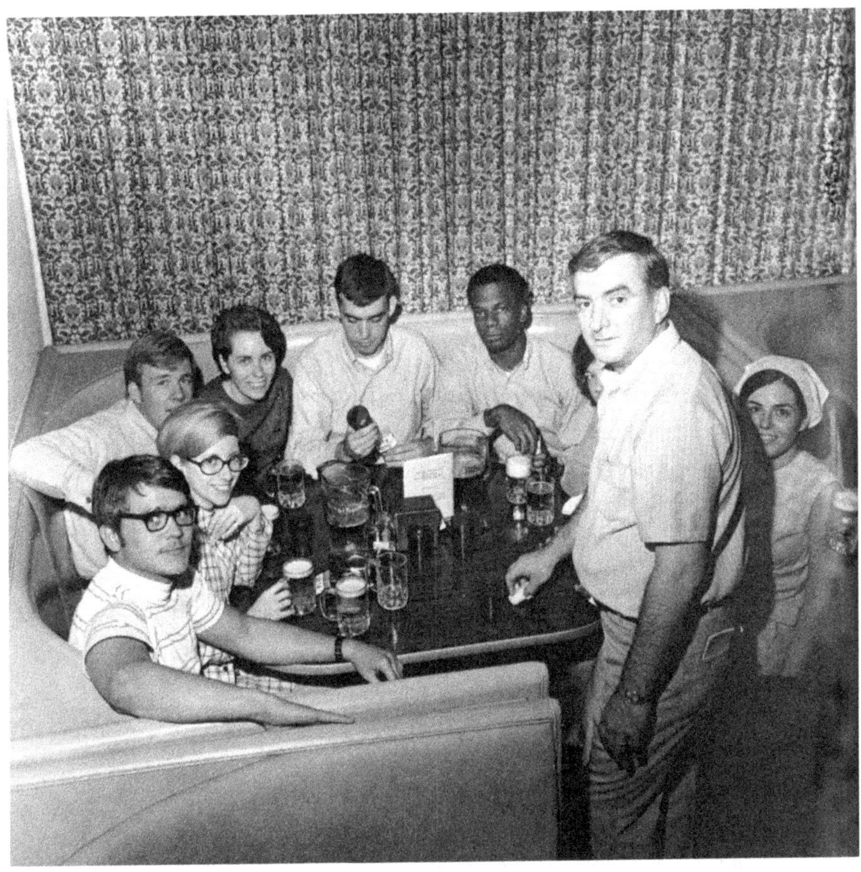

By 1969, African American students were allowed in most restaurants and movie theaters. Pat Martin, co-owner of the D-Lux, stops to talk with university students that year. Martin and his wife, Helen, ran the D-Lux on Dickson Street, expanding it to the game room on the east and eventually into its basement, where the Rathskeller offered a shrimp and oyster bar. *Courtesy Arkansas Razorback.*

evenly divided between boys and girls. Almost unanimously, the African American students wanted to live and work somewhere other than Fayetteville. As the report noted, some of that desire might be the desire of any restless teenager thinking about a better life elsewhere, but the reality of Fayetteville through at least the 1960s afforded very limited job opportunities for African Americans. The report noted: "That there is job discrimination against Negroes, in Fayetteville and elsewhere, is, of course, beyond question. The simple fact, for example, that there are no Negroes at all who are employed in any one of Fayetteville's industries is ample testimony to the point."[122]

Students also pointed to the lack of social amenities for African Americans in the community. Only two places—the Palace Drugstore and Woolworth's—allowed African Americans to be served at the counter. The public swimming pool, the public tennis courts, the roller skating rink—all were off limits. Of the three movie theaters, the Palace Theater allowed African Americans in the balcony, the Uark Theater allowed black university students and the Ozark Theater did not allow them at all. The students also perceived an inability to live where they wanted to live within the town even if they did have a good job. Would they be allowed to buy a house in a white neighborhood?

To test the extent to which this was true, a private group of university women called the World Affairs Group began working toward integration of the social and cultural organizations of the city, including the restaurants, theaters and parks. After incidents in Greensboro, North Carolina, in which a Woolworth's store refused to serve African American customers in 1960, the Fayetteville group ran a local test:

> *We had a Woolworth's downtown that had a lunch counter, and as far as we knew never had served blacks. Blacks never tried to go in there, I guess.... We had a couple of blacks and a couple of whites meet down there in front of Woolworth's and just go in and sit down at the counter and order some ice cream or something. And they were served. You know, nothing happened. And it was the kind of thing that we were delighted by, that nobody cared. So that, kind of, is the way Fayetteville is.*[123]

A number of local organizations took up the cause, including the Fayetteville Community Relations Association, the Arkansas Council on Human Relations, United Church Women and the League of Women Voters. They made recommendations, rather than demands, and eschewed the use of provocative or belligerent language in their communications with the school board. Theirs was the tactic of persistent pressure through rational discourse—a tactic that proved to be highly effective in achieving the objective of school desegregation without the acrimony and bitterness so evident in other communities.[124]

A Shift from Town to City

Ellen Compton, a director of the Washington County Historical Society, described the 1960s as the period when Fayetteville quit being a big town and became a small city. Her observation spoke not only to the physical place but also to the city policies and self-perception that residents had for Fayetteville.

One of the changes occurred in the structure of city government. At the urging of the League of Women Voters, city residents decided to switch from a mayor/council form of government to a city manager/board form in 1965. The former was the traditional municipal arrangement, with voters electing a mayor to oversee the city operations and a city council to develop ordinances. Major criticisms of this form were that mayors could be elected who turned out to have little understanding of city government or, in a worst-case scenario, that a mayor who relied on votes might succumb to favoritism or undue influence.

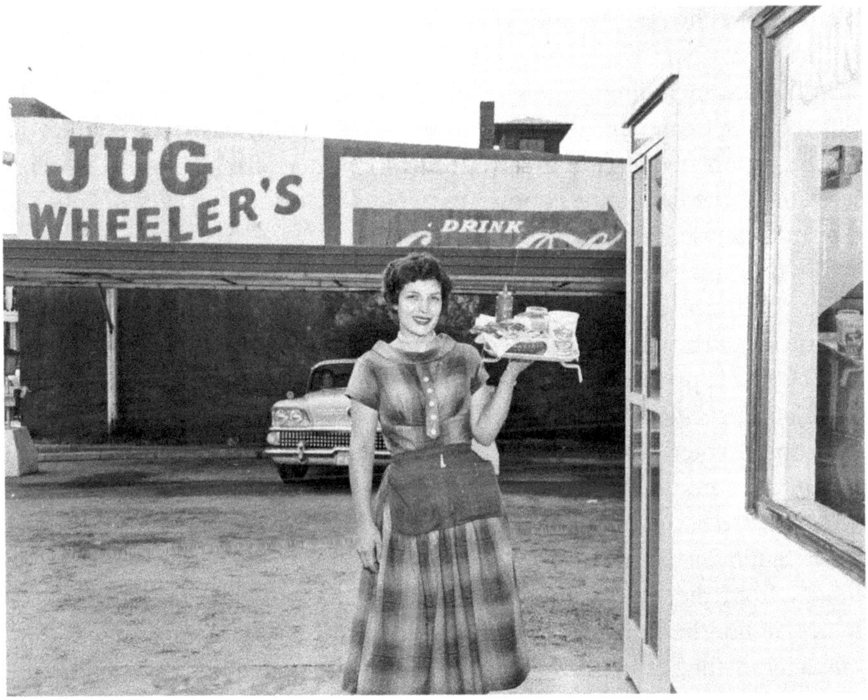

Arlen Kelly Stewart carries a tray of food at Jug Wheeler's Drive-In, a popular drive-in restaurant on Dickson Street in 1959. The present-day restaurant Bordino's covers the site of Jug's and incorporated part of the old drive-in into its building. *Courtesy* Northwest Arkansas Democrat-Gazette *and Shiloh Museum of Ozark History/*Northwest Arkansas Time *Collection, NWAT Box 4 4x5.74.*

Advocates for the city manager/board form of government argued that it would reduce those conflicts. A board of directors would be elected, and it would hire a professional city administrator to manage municipal operations. Fayetteville voters approved the change, including a provision that the seven-member board would then elect one of its members to serve as a ceremonial mayor who could represent the city at such events as ribbon cuttings and press conferences.

The physical city grew enormously, as new subdivisions sprang up and commercial operations spread along the entryways to the city. The city reported a near-doubling of value for building permits from 1963 to 1964, increasing from $2.9 million to $4.6 million.[125] Several manufacturers opened plants in Fayetteville during the 1950s and 1960s. Bear Brand Hosiery, for instance, announced that it would open a manufacturing plant at Fayetteville in 1950, initially employing one hundred people. Campbell Soup opened a major processing facility on Fifteenth Street. In 1958, the Baldwin Piano Company opened a 200,000-square-foot manufacturing plant on Beechwood Avenue, as well as two more in Arkansas, all managed by Stan Krueger. The plant manufactured a variety of electrical musical instruments, including organs, guitars and bass guitars. And in 1965, the Shakespeare Company, a manufacturer of fishing gear based in Kalamazoo, Michigan, opened a plant in Fayetteville to produce fishing reels. The plant was one of the first in the country to treat its factory wastewater on-site and filter it for reuse.

Building on that success, the city board voted the same year to use $250,000 from water and sewer revenues to fund creation of a 480-acre industrial park south of Fifteenth Street. The city money was put with $160,000 of private money raised by the chamber of commerce and $484,000 provided by the state Economic Development Administration. The board voted five to two for the project, a sign of dissent that existed within the community as well.

The board had previously put two ballot issues before voters to use property tax revenue for the same purpose, and voters turned down both. Providing money from the water and sewer fund rankled many residents, and more than one hundred turned out for the meeting. City Director James Kerlin, manager of the Standard Register printing plant and up for reelection, said, "I feel like I would be betraying you [the Fayetteville residents] if I did not use my best judgment and vote for it. As a plant manager, I should probably be against this because it will probably cost me money in higher wages. You can vote me out, but in my judgment it's in the best interest of Fayetteville."[126]

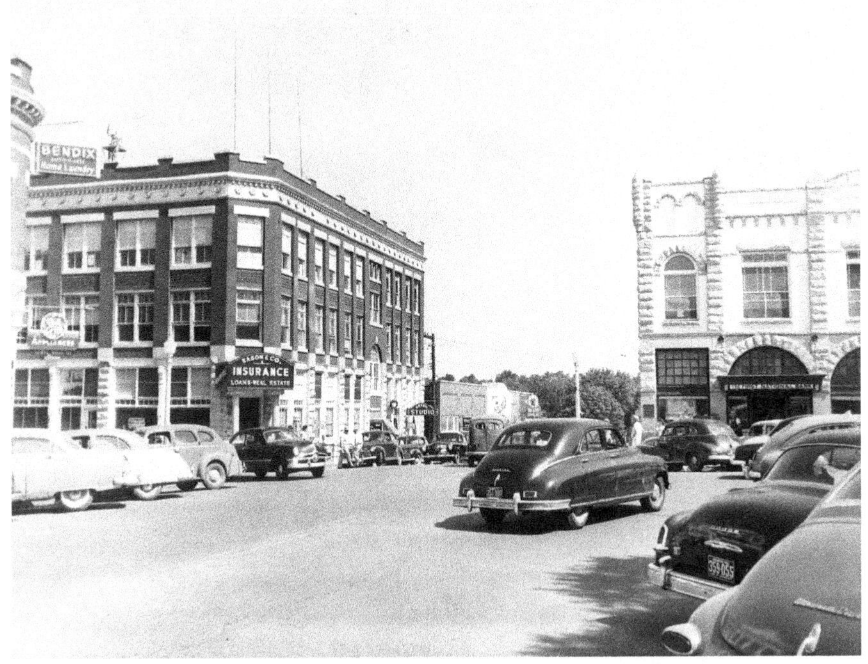

By 1952, the clapboard and frame buildings of the nineteenth century had been replaced by stately brick and stone structures. The northwest corner included the Eason Insurance Company; the First National Bank, *at right*; and Lewis Bros. Hardware, *at extreme left. Courtesy UA Libraries, William S. Campbell Collection, MC1427.*

Part of the decision was likely dictated by competition in the region. The nearby cities of Bentonville, Rogers, Siloam Springs and Springdale also sought to establish industrial parks, and Rogers succeeded quickly in drawing Emerson Electric Company to establish a plant at its park.[127]

In Fayetteville, the industrial park gained clients slowly over a thirty-year period but never reached its full potential. Nevertheless, companies such as Hiland Dairy, Superior Industries, Marshalltown Tools, the U.S. Postal Service and American Air Filter Company established successful and long-term manufacturing and processing facilities in the industrial park. By the 2010s, though, many acres remained pasture.

The early manufacturers were slowly displaced. Shakespeare eventually closed its rod and reel operation, but the plant became a home for one of Tyson Foods' processing facilities. Governor Bill Clinton was on hand to announce the operation in 1983. Tyson Foods, headquartered in Springdale just north of Fayetteville, was expanding its operations from

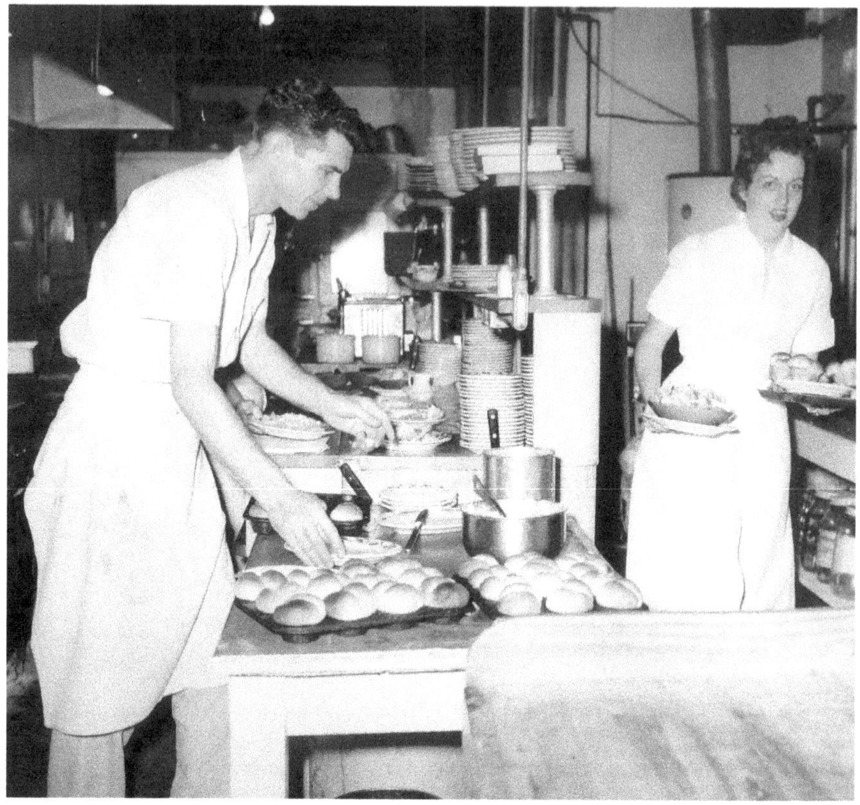

Arlis Wayne "Sarge" Hulse, *left*, and Bonnie Hoskins Capwell Brooks prepare food at the King Chicken Restaurant in January 1959. *Photo by Ray Watson. Courtesy Shiloh Museum of Ozark History, Ray Watkins Collection, S-2002-50-806.*

wholesale poultry marketing to a "vertically integrated" company. Along with growing poultry and processing birds for market, the company developed further processing opportunities with chain restaurants to supply specific products such as chicken nuggets or chicken fingers with specifications to match each restaurant's desires.

Bear Brand Hosiery lost business as the demand for nylon hose dropped. During the company's heyday, it did undergarment research at the Fayetteville plant that resulted in patents for all manner of improvements to the way undergarments were manufactured. Among them was a "one-piece seamless unidirectional rotary-knitted anti-embolism stocking," designed to prevent pooling of blood in the feet and ankles.[128]

After Bear Brand Hosiery closed its Fayetteville operation, the University of Arkansas acquired the property and opened an engineering experiment center that eventually became the Arkansas Research and Technology Park, a business incubator for fledgling technology companies, most of which spring from research being conducted at the university in such fields as solar power, wastewater treatment and the traditional electric grid.

Fayetteville and the university also saw another power partnership form in the mid-1970s. The school of law hired two law professors, Bill Clinton and Hillary Rodham, who lived just off campus after they were married in 1975 at a house that is now the Clinton House Museum.

The Rise of Ozark Modern

The rise in reputation of the University of Arkansas's program in architecture during the 1950s and 1960s also gave rise to a significant shift in Fayetteville's architecture.

Among the early architects in the Modern movement, Warren Segraves leaned toward the International style. He nearly always used exposed steel and swaths of glass in support of solid blocks of masonry that gave many of his buildings the look of a rectangular block floating detached from the ground, a nod to the German architect Ludwig Mies van der Rohe. Segraves's best-known works in Fayetteville are the Roberta Fulbright Building, which originally housed the Fayetteville Public Library, and the Southwest Electric Power Company Building, which now houses a bank at the northeast corner of College Avenue and Dickson Street.

Fayetteville's best-known architect at that time, native son Edward Durell Stone, had attended the university before an architecture program was created. He turned heads around the world, though, with his designs of the Museum of Modern Art in New York City; the U.S. Embassy in New Delhi, India; and the Kennedy Center for the Performing Arts in Washington, D.C. Stone returned to Fayetteville to design several buildings, including the Fine Arts Center at the University of Arkansas, the first educational center in the country to integrate the fine arts of music, theater, architecture and art into one building.[129] He also designed several residences in Arkansas, including the Willis Noll House on Mount Sequoyah, a building that fits within the Ozark Modern style.

Quite a few of the architecture professors during the 1950s and 1960s—Fay Jones, Herbert K. Fowler, Cyrus Sutherland and John Williams among them—were practicing architects as well, and many of them were influenced by the Prairie style of architecture developed by Frank Lloyd Wright, who spoke at the university in 1958. The Arkansas architects took Wright's ideas about form and function and gave them Ozarkian bones, using native materials to create a style that came to be known as Ozark Modern.

Jones, who apprenticed under Wright, led this movement. Instead of creating buildings detached from the earth, Jones designed architecture as a seemingly organic element of the building's place. Many of his residences were built from native stone and glass with low-slung cedar-shake roofs. Many of them hugged the hills, while others stood out from the crest of a hill as though they were part of a jutting sandstone bluff.

Jones's best-known work, Thorncrown Chapel in nearby Eureka Springs, was named the fourth-best design of a building during the twentieth century by the American Institute of Architects.[130]

The Ribbon of College Avenue

In 1960, the city's first shopping center, Evelyn Hills, named for Grace Evelyn Abshier, opened on College Avenue just north of Abshier Drive. Its opening marked the first in a commercial sprawl along North College Avenue in which small buildings with large parking lots sprang up: fast-food restaurants, banks, car lots, motels, shops and offices. It became known as "The Strip."

Evelyn Hills included a large grocery, a Sterling dime store, clothing stores, shoe stores, a McIlroy Bank branch drive-through and the Montgomery-Ward Department Store as an anchor. Tucked away were also service-oriented shops such as dentist offices and barbershops. The center turned the traditional Fayetteville Square on its head, putting parking at the center of everything and stretching the retail area in a long, sinuous line around the parking. Soon other smaller shopping centers popped up, from Oak Plaza on Garland Avenue to the East Gate and West Gate Shopping Centers on the southeast and southwest corners of town.

The development of College Avenue followed this example, developing as a long, thin commercial strip from downtown to the northern reaches of the city limits. The strip development meant that other parts of the city avoided some of the eyesores common along College. Gibson's Discount Center, for instance, left the square in 1963 to open a large store on College Avenue, promising more than three hundred parking spaces. The state widened

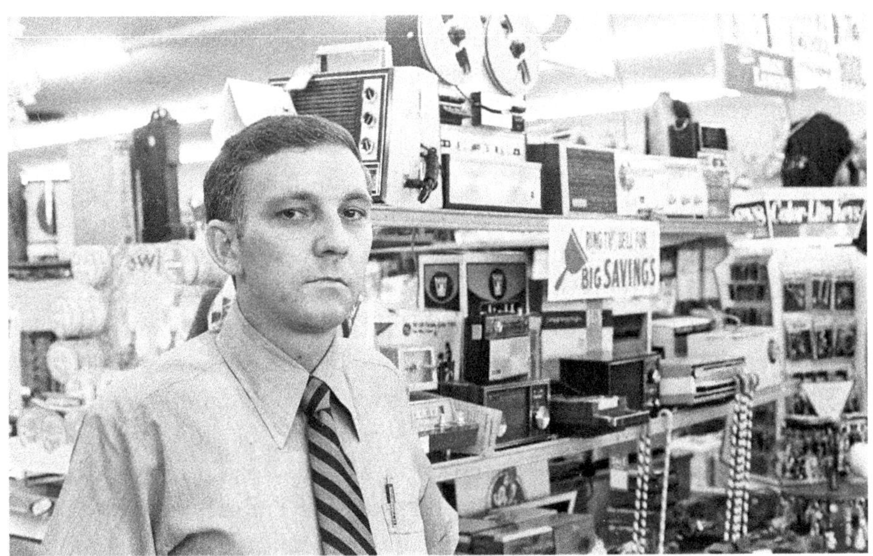

Glen E. Bewley, shown in August 1970, was the first manager of the Sterling Variety Store at Evelyn Hills when it opened in 1960. Sterling, an Arkansas chain based in Little Rock, provided everything from back-to-school necessities to tropical fish and hamsters for sale. *Courtesy* Northwest Arkansas Democrat-Gazette *and Shiloh Museum of Ozark History/* Northwest Arkansas Time *Collection, NWAT Box 22 70.1.*

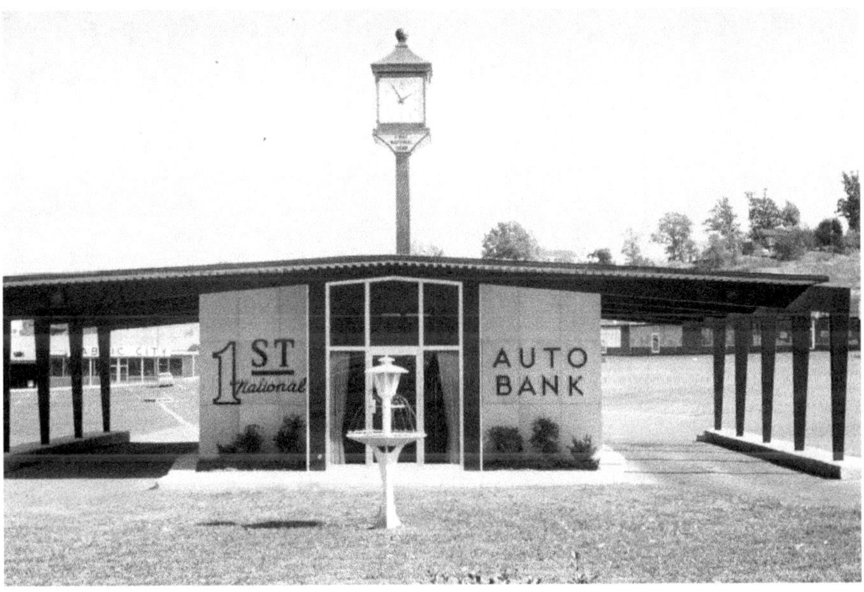

When Evelyn Hills Shopping Center opened in 1961, in addition to retail outlets, the center boasted a First National Bank drive-through branch. The highly modern styling of the branch bank clashed slightly with the very traditional clock patterned after the bank's clock on the Fayetteville Square. *Photo by Herbert K. Fowler.*

the highway during the 1970s, pushing curbs closer to existing businesses. More businesses opened in the remaining vacant spaces, creating a linear shopping center of sorts, leading to the newly built Northwest Arkansas Mall. In response to the helter-skelter development of the street, the city adopted a sign ordinance in 1972 to eliminate billboards within the city limits and reduce garish business signs. The city's planning department also adopted sweeping development standards to try to prevent similar injury to the beauty of other parts of the city.

By the 1970s, through-traffic along U.S. 71 had grown so intense that the state began building a bypass around the western edge of the city. The bypass was built to interstate standards, with divided northbound and southbound lanes from the intersection of School Avenue and Skelton Street on the south side of town to College Avenue near Millsap Road on the north. The City of Fayetteville named the new highway the Fulbright Expressway in honor of its most famous Fayetteville resident, Senator J. William Fulbright, a Democrat who sponsored legislation leading to the Fulbright Scholars program. After the bypass became part of Interstate 540, now I-49, the federal government named the interstate in honor of U.S. Representative

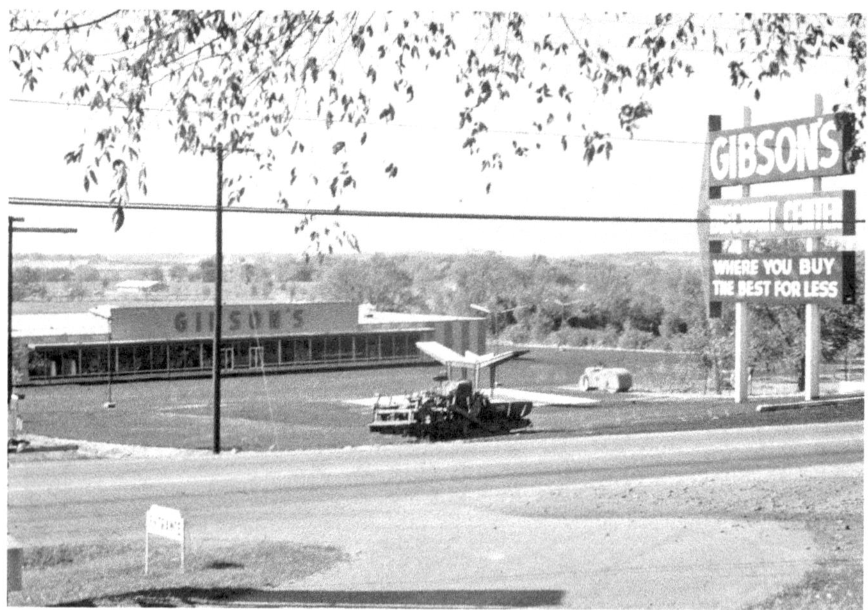

Gibson's Discount Center was the first "big box" store to open in Fayetteville. It led the migration of Fayetteville's retail businesses off of the square and north along College Avenue. Opening on October 23, 1963, Gibson's offered more than three hundred parking spaces. *Photo by Herbert K. Fowler.*

John Paul Hammerschmidt, a Republican. Fayetteville residents joked that the right lane of the bypass would be Hammerschmidt's, and the left lane would be Fulbright's.

In August 1971, Sears moved out of its narrow two-story store on Center Street and opened a new spacious store on a hilltop near the city boundary between Fayetteville and Springdale. It was the first "anchor" of a retail complex named the Northwest Arkansas Plaza, which colloquially became known as the Northwest Arkansas Mall. For its grand opening, Sears did its best to entreat customers:

> *Browse through Sears spacious new Northwest Arkansas Store—a wonder-world of shopping excitement.*
>
> *Throughout this luxurious complex you'll find unique specialty shops that reflect the singular creative talents of the Sears designers. Meet us on the red carpet of our bold Men's store....In the pastel fairy-plush, golden playground of our children's department that is guarded by "Winnie the Pooh."*
>
> *Remember that Sears has everything for your home, too. Visit our improvement headquarters or talk with our home decorator consultants. Aisles of fine furniture and appliances await your inspection.*[131]

The Sears store represented a major shift in Fayetteville's retail landscape and the first inkling of Fayetteville's role as a leader in development of a regional identity. Instead of a small store, the new Sears was the size of a warehouse and included numerous departments and services. And instead of small stores gathered around an outdoor square with limited parking, the new Northwest Arkansas Plaza gathered more than fifty-five stores within an air-conditioned building under one roof.[132]

The rest of the mall was built to the north of Sears and opened with forty-five thousand square feet of floor space, beginning in March 1972 with Dillard's department store anchoring the north end. Between them were Woolworth's, the Mall Twin Cinema, a First Federal Savings branch, Bed & Bath Fashion Shop, Mr. Dees Shoes, Osco Drugs, Perry's Jewelry, John's Jeans, Gordon's Jewelry, Bresler's Ice Cream Shop, Heritage Books, Karmelkorn, Trumbo's Clothing Shop, Plaza Liquor, Bowen's Restaurant, A.G. Edwards, Neff's and the Oxford Shop, among others. During the intervening years, the mall expanded, adding a major wing to the west that doubled its size and remains anchored by J.C. Penney.

Built at the heart of the mall was the Boston Store, the most fashionable clothing store on Fayetteville's Square from the 1920s on. Like Woolworth's,

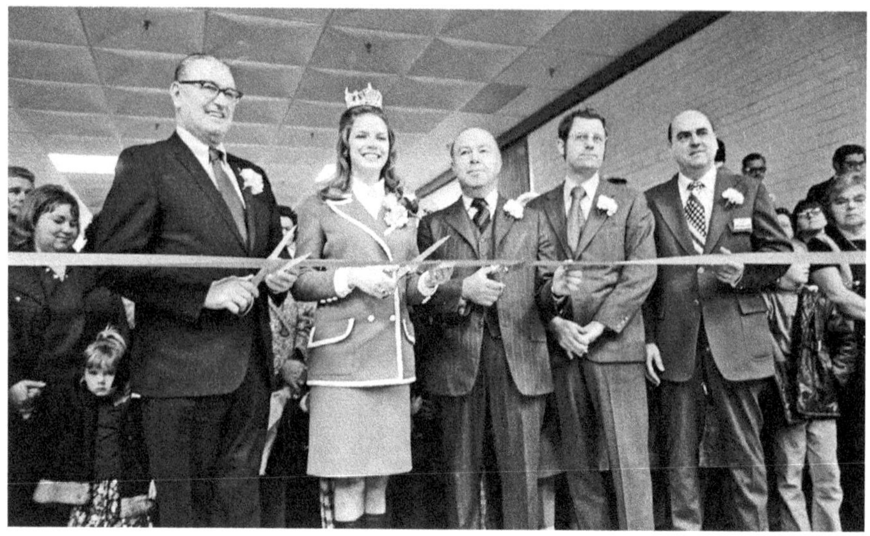

Dignitaries from across the region were on hand to cut the ribbon for the grand opening of the Northwest Arkansas Plaza on March 2, 1972. *From left to right*: Vice-Mayor Ernest Lancaster; Miss Arkansas Marilyn Morgan; Martin Buckshaum, chair of the board for developer General Growth Properties; Lee Taylor of Rogers; and Lee Zachary of the Springdale Chamber of Commerce. *Photo by Ken Good. Courtesy* Northwest Arkansas Democrat-Gazette, *Shiloh Museum of Ozark History, Springdale News Collection, SN 3-2-1972.*

Penney and Sears, the Boston Store opened a new store at the Northwest Arkansas Plaza. Unlike the management of the other stores, though, the Boston Store's managers, Tom and Doris Hendricks, made a decision initially to keep open their store on the square. Tom noted in an interview:

> *The Square in downtown Fayetteville has been the hub and core of activity for too many years to just have it pass out of existence. The backdrop of the mountains against the town Square has made one of the most picturesque areas in the nation. The tower of Old Main can be seen from the Main Street. The Square is within easy walking distance for hundreds and is easily accessible to many more living in that direction of downtown Fayetteville.*

Hendricks's reference to "walking distance" proved anachronistic. The residents of Fayetteville were now traveling by automobile, and walking distance was merely a measure of how close a parking lot and open space were to the intended commercial destination.

The flight of retail stores from the Fayetteville Square and the aging quality of many of the buildings left it looking run-down. Federal "urban renewal" funding was secured to redevelop parts of the square, primarily the east side and northeast corners. The east side was demolished for construction of a new First National Bank location running the width of the block. On the north side, the century-old McIlroy Bank was torn down to build a new monolithic McIlroy Bank.

The post office at the center of the square, having been vacated by the U.S. Postal Service, was slated to be razed with an open pedestrian mall planned for the square. Residents, however, argued that enough destruction had happened and that the well-constructed building should be saved and given a continuing public use. The city worked out a deal to retain the grounds but sell the structure to the Bumpass family, which turned the post office into a restaurant and private club called the Old Post Office Gathering Place.

The Fayetteville Farmers' Market was established in 1973. Farmers from across the region could bring crops directly to the square for sale on Saturday mornings. Over the course of the next forty years, the market expanded to offer sales on Tuesday and Thursday mornings and a wider variety of materials than fresh produce. In 2012, the American Farmland Trust ranked the Fayetteville Farmers' Market no. 5 in the nation. At the turn of the twenty-first century, Fayetteville began appearing near the top of every imaginable national ranking: best place to raise a family, to work, to own a small business, to live, to retire and more.

In the early 2000s, the city under Mayor Dan Coody made its first attempt to restore some of College Avenue to its early luster by adding streetlamps and trees along the avenue from Meadow Street to Maple Street. In 2015, the city embarked on ways to improve the next section north, between Maple Street and North Street, looking for ways to calm traffic, increase pedestrian safety and beautify the streetscape.

The city also celebrated the opening of one of its most beautiful public buildings in 2004 when the Fayetteville Public Library cut the ribbon on the new Blair Library Building, designed by architect Jeffrey Scherer and named the national Library of the Year by *Library Journal* and Thompson/Gale Publishers in 2005.[133]

Two Wheels on Razorback Greenway

The city's hilliness made bicycling difficult even when following the best of routes. Nevertheless, bicycling in Fayetteville began in the late nineteenth century at least a decade before the first automobiles appeared. Mack McRoy received a tricycle in 1878: "Mack was the envy of all Fayetteville children as he pedaled his new volicipede on the board sidewalks of College avenue," Walter J. Lemke wrote. Fay Reed and Jo Harrison bought identical "penny-farthings" in the late nineteenth century. "Reed and Harrison staged an exhibition bicycle race on College avenue one day that ended with both riders taking inglorious head dives over the handlebars."[134]

In 1930, a bicycle derby between Fayetteville and Bentonville attracted twenty entrants, including one woman, Ethel Toney of Elkins. Each of the riders left the Fayetteville Square five minutes apart and followed the "hardtop" of U.S. 71. During World War II, when gasoline was being rationed, the Arkansas Western Gas Company sent its meter readers out by bicycle to check on residential usage. By the 1960s, students from grade school age to college age rode bicycles to class each day.

In 1971, the Society for Environmental Stabilization, the Ozark Society and the University Cycling Club sponsored a Hike or Bike Week. David Johnson, president of the former, noted:

> *It is hoped that citizens will forego the use of automobiles during the week to develop new habits of transportation for the sake of cleaner air and reduced traffic congestion. It is recognized that vehicular traffic is one of the leading contributors to air pollution and that the week will demonstrate the physiological and psychological benefits of walking or bicycling.*[135]

Interest continued to grow in bicycling as an alternative mode of transportation. In 1976, a subcommittee on parks, recreation and bikeways held a public meeting attended by more than fifty people, most of whom were interested in developing better bikeways, especially bike lanes on existing streets and highways. Chair Beverly Melton told the newspaper, "I think we had a lot of people there for the bikeways that wouldn't have come just for parks and recreation."[136]

A bicycle task force was created in 1980, and Mark Widder of Highroller Cyclery served on the task force and wrote a grant application to the Federal Highway Department that provided $15,000 to come up with a master plan. Two students studying landscape architecture at the University of Arkansas took up the project to determine Fayetteville's bicycle needs and develop a master bike plan: "People ride bicycles in Fayetteville for recreation, transportation and physical fitness and the biggest complaint seems to be

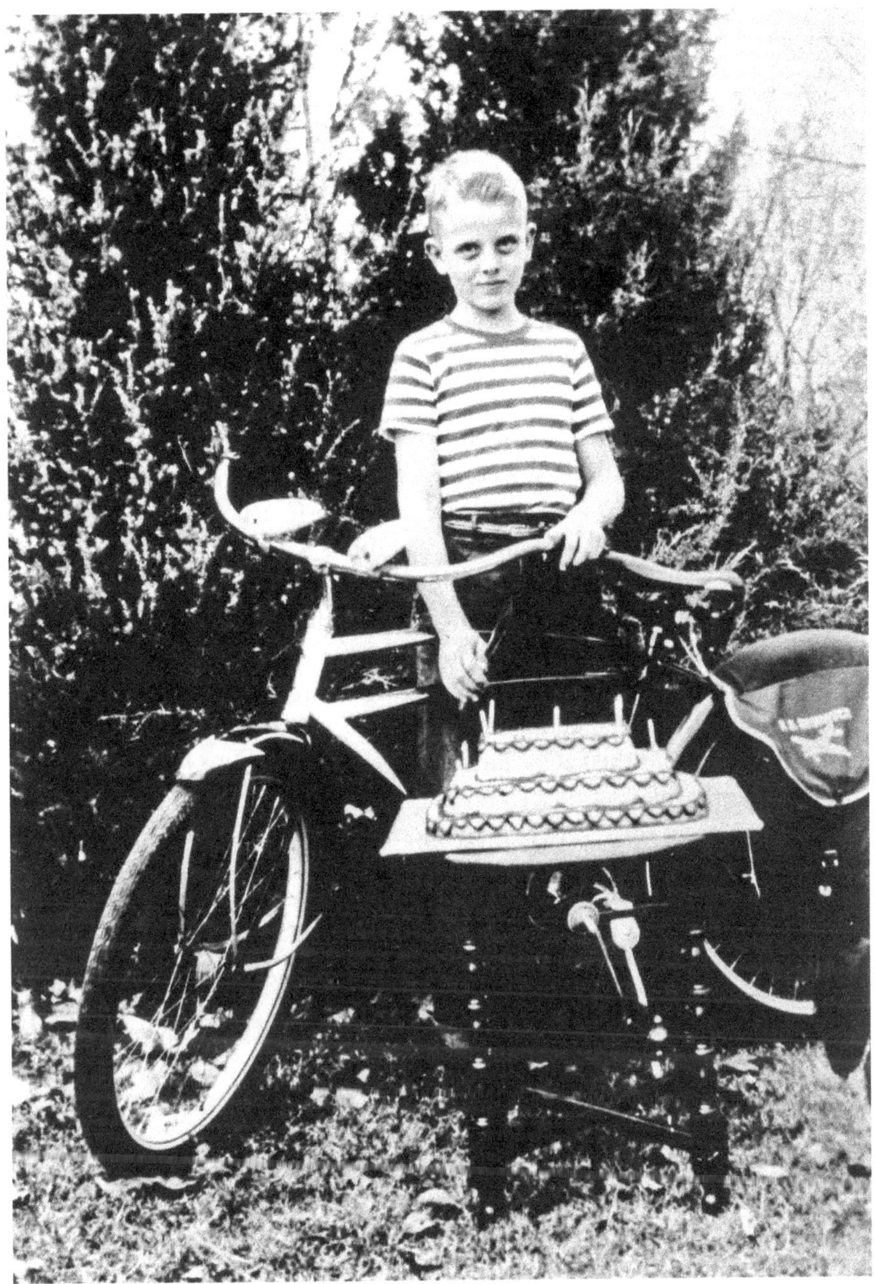

Orville Hall with his birthday cake and the bicycle he purchased from Montgomery Ward Department Store, pictured in from of Leverett Elementary School on October 30, 1946. *Courtesy Shiloh Museum of Ozark History, Orville and Susan Hall Collection, S-2009-60-24.*

that there is no safe place to ride. You have to go pretty far outside town to find a place to ride."

The task force's work resulted in a city map that color-coded streets and highways from relatively safe and easy streets to traffic-filled roads that should be avoided. The city also established bicycle routes through the town, posting bicycle route signs along streets that were less traveled by motor vehicles and usually flatter.

In the early 1990s, Mayor Fred Hanna created a bicycle committee that began developing a master trail plan, similar to the city's master street plan. When new developments came forward that were on or near the proposed corridors of bicycle trails, the city worked with the developers to set aside right of way for a path. The city's first bicycle path, Mud Creek Trail, came about when the CMN Business Park was developed south of the Northwest Arkansas Mall. Subsequently, the city built the first portion of the Frisco Trail between Center Street and Martin Luther King Boulevard.

In 2006, the city proposed three sales taxes, one for a new sewer plant, one for streets and a 0.25 percent sales tax to be dedicated to trail construction. The trails portion passed by the widest margin and provided $2.1 million of funding during the initial year, resulting in creation of the Scull Creek Trail, a north–south backbone for Fayetteville's trail system. Under Mayor Lioneld Jordan and the trails administrator, Matt Mihalevich, the city had paved more than forty miles of bicycle trails by 2015, and in May of that year, Scull Creek Trail, Frisco Trail and half of the Lake Fayetteville Trail became a part of the Razorback Greenway, a thirty-seven-mile regional trail from Lake Bentonville on the north end to Fayetteville's Walker Park on the south end.

Arts and Retail

Fayetteville voters approved a 1 percent tax on revenues of hotels, motels and restaurants in 1977 to pay for construction of a continuing education center at the northeast corner of the Fayetteville Square. The center provided the University of Arkansas with classroom space devoted to training of professionals who needed to stay current with licensing and latest practices, a closed-circuit television system that offered distance education to satellite classrooms across Arkansas and offices to oversee traditional correspondence courses and general extension education.

The new center would also provide conference and convention space for the adjacent Hilton Hotel, the city's first high-rise hotel. The influx of visitors for conferences and the taxes they paid for lodging and meals, in essence, paid for the center. Over the years, more restaurants and hotels opened in Fayetteville, increasing annual revenue from the hotel/motel/restaurant tax to more than $600,000 by 1992. The extra revenue could only be used for limited reasons: promotion of the city's tourism, funding of events likely to bring in tourists and financing of buildings such as the Continuing Education Center to bring in more visitors.[137]

Arkansas passed legislation in 1981 to allow cities and counties to seek approval of local general sales taxes. Washington County voters approved a 1 percent sales tax that year, the revenues of which were split between the county and cities based on a pro-rata formula. Fayetteville had used property tax to fund city government prior to that. During one of its sales tax elections, the city agreed to reduce its millage if voters would approve a sales tax, and they did.

Desires of the city for a community-based arts and theater facility and by the University of Arkansas for a major performance facility came together in 1992 with construction of the Walton Arts Center. The city used part of its extra revenues to finance bonds to pay for Fayetteville's share of the cost of building the arts center in 1992. The University of Arkansas used a major gift from the Walton Family Charitable Support Foundation to cover its share, but the facility that leaders envisioned would cost even more. Billie Jo Starr proved to be the central leader in the project:

> *Sam Walton,* [the founder of Walmart Stores], *really encouraged us to get a lot of different people involved in the project. We began hosting in-home community parties. The host would invite their friends, and we would come and bring the model and share the vision. We were not directly asking for money, we were sharing information. Later we made the follow up calls.*[138]

And the calls were answered. Smaller donations from people across Northwest Arkansas provided another $7 million to allow the facility to open debt-free on day one. The six-hundred-seat facility built on Dickson Street brought in the top Broadway touring performances and created performance spaces for such local organizations as Arts Live Theatre, the Northwest Arkansas Jazz Society, University Theatre, the Northwest Arkansas Symphony and eventually TheatreSquared, the national award-winning professional company based in Fayetteville today.

The Walton Arts Center also sparked a revival of development along Dickson Street, a landmark for visitors to Fayetteville. The city used federal funding to redevelop the street and sidewalks, narrowing the trafficway while expanding pedestrian right of ways. Flower beds and trees were planted from College Avenue to Arkansas Avenue. In turn, private property owners began renovating, redesigning and rebuilding their own businesses. Today, the street is known as the entertainment district of the state. Motorcyclists infest it during the Bikes, Blues & Barbecue event; a half dozen parades float through its sea; the Joe Martin Bicycle Stage Race and the Hogeye Marathon routinely include it on their race routes; and Razorback fans throng to the bars and restaurants to celebrate another victory or drown in their hogwallow.

The growth in the city also meant a growth among religious groups that had been small minorities. Adherents in Unitarianism and Universalism joined forces in 1961 to create the Unitarian Universalist Fellowship and built a church south of the university campus. The Jewish community had had a presence in Fayetteville since soon after the Civil War but didn't have a strong enough population until 1981 to form the Temple Shalom of Northwest Arkansas. The Church of Jesus Christ of Latter-day Saints likewise had followers in Fayetteville who met informally during the 1950s and 1960s but didn't have a large enough congregation until the 1970s to build a meetinghouse.

Funky Fayetteville

In May 2000, a fifty-three-year-old grandmother named Mary Lightheart climbed into an oak tree at the site of a proposed shopping center on the north side of town. The oak tree was one among a large grove of ancient trees, a grove that existed amid the prairie before the lines on the map were drawn. The Fayetteville City Council had given the developers permission to cut down most of the grove, and Lightheart's ascension into the limbs of one tree was a last-ditch effort to protest the decision, seen by her adherents as a violation of the city's tree-preservation ordinance. During the next three weeks, the protest would spread to the courts, where at one point legal cases were being argued in every court available.

Municipal court was filled with cases of misdemeanor civil disobedience trespassers; the circuit court heard an appeal of the Fayetteville City Council's decision; in chancery court, Lightheart's ex-husband made a filing to require her to appear for an unrelated issue; and federal court heard arguments related to whether the removal of the trees would affect a migratory pair of hawks. Lightheart was eventually arrested for trespass while trying to return to her tree after appearing in the chancery court case. The other court cases were resolved, and the development went forward.[139]

The protest, whether one agrees with its means or intended ends, remains a touchstone for a citizenry that values public involvement and resolution of issues in the common marketplace of ideas. Fayetteville residents had created their form of city government and were capable of re-forming it. The tree-preservation ordinance was reworked by a committee of residents to resolve some of the issues brought to light during the tree saga.

Quality of life for most residents continues to play a higher moral role than the simpler economic ethos of progress at any cost. Perhaps the central expression of that ethos is the garden at the center of the Square, a floral magnet for tourists and locals who visit the Farmers' Market, alive with the seasonal color of blooms and blossoms through the summer and shimmering with a million flickers of light during winter's Lights of the Ozarks. A quirky quality of life, as it turned out, continued to draw retail, housing and commercial investment during the twenty-first century. A minor campaign in the 1990s to market Fayetteville as "Fantastic" was quietly dropped after a local business started printing bumper stickers that read, "Keep Fayetteville Funky."

NOTES

Chapter 1

1. Mathews, *Talking to the Moon*, 33–34.

Chapter 2

2. *History of Benton*, 228.
3. Brue, "Amerique Septentrionale 3," 29; Arrowsmith and Von Humboldt, *New Map of Mexico and Adjacent Provinces*, 11.
4. Campbell, *One Hundred Years of Fayetteville*, 5.
5. J.H. Van Hoose, *Fayetteville Democrat*, July 3, 1928.
6. Hildreth, *Dragoon Campaign to the Rocky Mountains*, 74.
7. Fayetteville History website, "Announcement of Initial Sale of Town Lots," http://www.fayettevillehistory.com/primary/2009/12/index.html.
8. *Arkansas Gazette*, "Lawrence County Democratic Nominations," June 14, 1836.
9. *Arkansas State Gazette*, May 30, 1838.
10. *Arkansas State Gazette*, April 26, 1836.
11. Hallum, *Biographical and Pictorial History of Arkansas*, 117; *Northwest Arkansas Times*, July 18, 1940.
12. Meek, "Live of Archibald Yell," 353–79.
13. Michael B. Dougan, "David Walker," Encyclopedia of Arkansas History & Culture.

14. Walker, *Address of Hon. David Walker.*
15. Lemke, *Early Colleges and Academies*, 10. This publication is also listed as no. 6 in the society's Bulletin Series.
16. U.S. Fish and Wildlife Service, "The Trail of Tears National Historic Trail and the Tennessee, Wheeler and White River National Wildlife Refuges: Historical and Interpretation Study"; Heritage Trail Partners website, "Mount Comfort," http://www.heritagetrailpartners.com/2015/05/mount-comfort.
17. Rhea, *Thirty Years in Arkansas*, 26.
18. James P. Neal, "The Arrington and Wallace War," *Flashback* (January 1956): 29.
19. William Isaac Irvine Morrow, unpublished diary, a portion of which was reproduced in *Flashback* (July 1957): 1–2.
20. Cherokee Nation website, "Parties Leaving Under Their Own Supervision," http://www.cherokee.org/AboutTheNation/History/TrailofTears/Partiesleavingundertheirownsupervision.aspx.
21. Neal, "Arrington and Wallace War," 29.
22. Worley, "Story of Alfred W. Arrington," 320–22.
23. Neal, "Arrington and Wallace War," 30–31.
24. *Arkansas Gazette*, April 1, 1840.
25. Castelow, "Miss Sophia Sawyer," 188–89.
26. Lemke, *Early Colleges and Academies*, 37–40.
27. *Witness*, February 6, 1841.
28. Little, "Noted Daughters of Arkansas."
29. *Flashback*, "Studying Under Sophia Sawyer" (February 1976): 32.
30. Michael Dougan, "Far West Seminary," Encyclopedia of Arkansas History & Culture.
31. *History of Benton*, 242–43.
32. Grayson, *Creek Warrior for the Confederacy*, 52.
33. Baxter, *Pea Ridge and Prairie Grove*, vii.
34. Ragland, "Arkansas College."
35. Grayson, *Creek Warrior for the Confederacy*, 52
36. Baxter, *Pea Ridge and Prairie Grove*, 31.
37. *Fayetteville Democrat*, "Four Coaches, 18 Horses Stabled in Fayetteville," Centennial Edition, July 3, 1828.
38. Ibid.
39. Franks, "California Overland Express," 77.
40. Ormsby, *Butterfield Overland Mail*, 5.
41. Franks, "California Overland Express," 76–77.

42. Sam Marrs to Sam Alexander, letter reprinted in *Flashback* (November 1957): 15–16.
43. Lemke, *Early Colleges and Academies*, 77.
44. Elias C. Boudinot, letter to the *Fayetteville Democrat*, January 13, 1872, 2.
45. *New York Times*, "Weather at Fayetteville, Arkansas," November 2, 1860.
46. *Northwest Arkansas Times Sesqui-Centennial Edition*, "Standards High at City Seminary," July 16, 1978. Newspaper clipping in Sophia Sawyer Vertical File, Special Collections, University of Arkansas Libraries, Fayetteville.

Chapter 3

47. *Arkansian*, March 5, 1859.
48. *Arkansian*, February 1, 1861.
49. *Arkansian*, March 30, 1860.
50. *New York Times*, April 9,1861.
51. Baxter, *Pea Ridge and Prairie Grove*, 39–40.
52. *War Bulletin*, January 9, 1862.
53. Yeater, "My Experiences During the War Between the States," 11.
54. Baxter, *Pea Ridge and Prairie Grove*, 50.
55. Ibid., 56–57.
56. Ibid., 58.
57. *History of Benton*, 228.
58. *Boston Morning Journal*, January 27, 1863.
59. Baxter, *Pea Ridge and Prairie Grove*, 135.
60. Baker and Baker, *WPA Oklahoma Slave Narratives*, 397–405.
61. Ibid.
62. Cornish, *Sable Arm*, 147.
63. *War of the Rebellion: A Compilation of the Official Records of the Union and Confederate Armies*, ser. 1, vol. 22, pt. 2, 192.
64. Bishop, *Loyalty on the Frontier*, 210–11.
65. E.D. Harrison, "The Battle of Fayetteville," *Flashback* 18 (April 1968): 17.
66. Cabell's report was written from Ozark on April 25, 1863, to Colonel S.S. Anderson, adjutant general of the district of Arkansas.
67. Yeater, "My Experiences During the War Between the States," 20–21.
68. Mahan, *Battle of Fayetteville, Arkansas*, 36.
69. Ibid., 44–48.
70. Richard Bland, "Marcus Larue Harrison," Encyclopedia of Arkansas History & Culture.

71. *Missouri Democrat*, "Col. Brooks's Investment of that Post," November 14, 1864.
72. Brock, *Southern Historical Society Papers.*
73. Ibid.
74. *Missouri Democrat*, "Col. Brooks's Investment of that Post."
75. Pat Donat, "Fagan's Attack on Fayetteville," *Flashback* 35, no. 4: 8–13. This article originally appeared in the *Northwest Arkansas Times* in 1985.
76. Ibid.

Chapter 4

77. *Fayetteville Weekly Democrat,* July 17, 1868.
78. Walter J. Lemke, "The Henderson School in Fayetteville," *Flashback* (May 1967): 1.
79. *Flashback*, "Henderson School: Then and Now" (August 1977): 47–48; Kim Allen Scott, "War and Remembrance: Reconstruction-Era Conflict in Washington County, Arkansas," *Flashback* (Fall 2013): 105–6.
80. Alvord, *Tenth Semi-Annual Report on Schools*, 41.
81. F.S. Root, "The Old Henderson School," *Flashback* (March 1954): 4.
82. Campbell, *One Hundred Years of Fayetteville*, 56.
83. Bureau of Census, "Thirteenth Census of the United States, 134.
84. *Fayetteville Daily Democrat*, August 13, 1915, 2; August 17, 1917, 1.
85. *Fayetteville Daily Democrat*, May 22, 1934, 1; September 3, 1936, 1.
86. Charles Alison, "Betty Davis: Building a Board from Splinters," *Flashback* 62, no. 3: 122–41.
87. Members of the Washington County Retired Teachers Association, *School Days, School Days*, 53.
88. Ibid.
89. Campbell, *One Hundred Years of Fayetteville*, 56.
90. *Northwest Arkansas Times*, "Railroad Ends Passenger Run Through City," September 18, 1965.
91. *New York Times*, September 7, 1886.
92. *New York Times*, April 15, 1903.
93. *Northwest Arkansas Times*, "Railroad Ends Passenger Run Through City."
94. *St. Louis Globe-Democrat*, April 22, 1880.
95. Edward A. Vandeventer, "Fayetteville Incidents of Seventy Years Ago," *Flashback* (August 1957): 29–30.

96. *Flashback* 61, no. 1, "Fayetteville's Water System on the West Fork of the White River" (Spring 2011): 3–23.
97. Letter from J.W.K. to Friend Billy, dated Fayetteville, October 16, 1878. Copy in author's collection.
98. *New-York Weekly Times*, April 2, 1879, 5.

Chapter 5

99. *New York Times*, November 28 and 29, 1905.
100. Thaden, *High, Wide and Frightened*, 78.
101. Members of the Washington County Retired Teachers Association, *School Days, School Days*, 107.
102. Campbell, *One Hundred Years of Fayetteville*, 56.
103. Members of the Washington County Retired Teachers Association, *School Days, School Days*, 97.
104. Ibid., 121–22.
105. *Northwest Arkansas Times*, "Enrollment of 3,000 Expected in Fayetteville," August 28, 1951, 1.
106. Edward Forrest Ellis, "I Remember," *Flashback* (May 1957): 33–34.
107. *Fayetteville Democrat*, "Arkansas Must Get Busy," January 3, 1916.
108. *Fayetteville Democrat*, November 27, 1917, 2.
109. *Fayetteville Democrat*, September 19, 1919, 1.
110. *Fayetteville Democrat*, August 1, 1924, 2.
111. Wappel and Garrison, *On the Avenue*, 3.
112. *Northwest Arkansas Times*, June 12, 1952, 7; June 11, 1952, 4; August 19, 1.
113. Mount Sequoyah, "History of Mount Sequoyah Retreat Center," http://mountsequoyah.org/history.
114. *Fayetteville Daily Democrat*, "Bankers Believe Plans Will 'Clarify,'" March 9, 1933. 1.
115. Dew, "New Deal and Fayetteville, Arkansas," 385.
116. *Daily Democrat*, February 21, 1934, 1; March 26, 1936, 1.
117. *Daily Democrat*, February 8, 1934, 1.
118. *Daily Democrat*, January 17, 1934, 1.
119. Dew, "New Deal and Fayetteville, Arkansas," 19.
120. Don Schaefer, "History of Buildings at the University of Arkansas," unpublished manuscript in author's collection.

Chapter 6

121. Methodist Commission on Christian Social Concern, "Report on the Outlook and Attitudes," 2–3.
122. Ibid., 3–5.
123. Adams and DeBlack, *Civil Obedience*, 156.
124. Ibid., 22.
125. *Northwest Arkansas Times*, January 8, 1965.
126. Tom Keith, *Northwest Arkansas Times*, October 19, 1968, 1.
127. *Northwest Arkansas Times*, March 6, 1965, 1; June 19, 1965, 1; September 18, 1965, 17; September 29, 1965, 7.
128. U.S. Patent 4,180,065, "Anti-Embolism Stocking," issued to Omer J. Bowen on January 23, 1978.
129. Encyclopedia of Arkansas History & Culture, "Warren Dennis Segraves."
130. Roy Reed, "Fay Jones, 83, Architect Influenced by Wright, Dies," *New York Times*, September 1, 2004.
131. *Northwest Arkansas Times*, August 18, 1971, 2.
132. *Northwest Arkansas Times*, January 18, 1972, 14.
133. Fayetteville Public Library, "Library History," http://www.faylib.org/content/library-history.
134. Patti Besom and Bob Besom, "Derby Served as Many Resident's Introduction to Bicycles," *Northwest Arkansas Times*, October 5, 2008.
135. *Northwest Arkansas Times*, October 19, 1971.
136. *Northwest Arkansas Times*, September 20, 1976.
137. Phyllis Rice, "Burger Tax a Big-Ticket Item for City," *Northwest Arkansas Times*, December 21, 1992, 1.
138. Walton Arts Center, "Mission and History," http://waltonartscenter.org/about/general-information/mission-and-history.
139. Laura Kellams, Joel Kirkland and Robert Smith, *Arkansas Democrat-Gazette*; Charles Alison, *Morning News of Northwest Arkansas*, May 9–31, 2000.

SELECTED BIBLIOGRAPHY

Adams, Julianne L., and Thomas A. DeBlack. *Civil Obedience: An Oral History of School Desegregation in Fayetteville, Arkansas, 1954–1965*. Fayetteville: University of Arkansas Press, 1994.

Alison, Charles Y., and Ellen K. Compton. *Images of America: Fayetteville.* Charleston, SC: Arcadia Publishing, 2011.

Alvord, J.W. *Tenth Semi-Annual Report on Schools for Freedmen*, July 1, 1870. Washington, D.C.: Government Printing Office, 1870.

Arrowsmith, Aaron, and Alexander von Humboldt. *A New Map of Mexico and Adjacent Provinces Compiled from Original Documents by A. Arrowsmith, 1810*. London, A. Arrowsmith: 1810.

Baker, T. Lindsay, and Julia P. Baker, eds. *The WPA Oklahoma Slave Narratives*. Norman: University of Oklahoma Press, 1996.

Baxter, William. *Pea Ridge and Prairie Grove, or Scenes and Incidents of the War in Arkansas.* Cincinnati, OH: Poe & Hitchcock, 1864.

Bishop, Albert W. *Loyalty on the Frontier; or, Sketches of the Union Men of the South-West*. St. Louis, MO: E.P. Studley, 1863.

Brock, R.A., ed. *Southern Historical Society Papers.* Richmond: Virginia Historical Society, 1876.

Brown, Kent R. *Fayetteville: A Pictorial History.* Norfolk, VA: Donning Company, 1982.

Brue, Adrien Hubert. *Amerique Septentrionale 3*. Paris: Desray, Libraire-Editeur, 1815.

Bureau of Census. "Thirteenth Census of the United States Taken in the Year 1910, Vol. II." Washington, D.C.: Government Printing Office, 1913.

Campbell, William S. *One Hundred Years of Fayetteville: 1828–1928*. Fayetteville, AR, 1928.

Castelow, Teri L. "Miss Sophia Sawyer: Founder of the Fayetteville Female Seminary." *Arkansas Historical Quarterly* 68, no. 2 (Summer 2009): 188–89.

Cornish, Dudley Taylor. *The Sable Arm*. Lawrence: University Press of Kansas, 1987.

Dew, Stephen H. "The New Deal and Fayetteville, Arkansas, 1933–1941." MA thesis, University of Arkansas, 1987.

The Encyclopedia of Arkansas History & Culture. Central Arkansas Library System. www.encyclopediaofarkansas.net.

Franks, Kenny, ed. "The California Overland Express through Indian Territory and Western Arkansas." *Arkansas Historical Quarterly* 33, no. 1 (Spring 1974).

Grayson, G.W. *A Creek Warrior for the Confederacy: The Autobiography of Chief G. W. Grayson*. Norman: University of Oklahoma Press, 1988.

Hallum, John. *Biographical and Pictorial History of Arkansas*. New York, 1887.

Hildreth, James. *Dragoon Campaign to the Rocky Mountains*. New York: Wiley & Long, 1836.

History of Benton, Washington, Carroll, Madison, Crawford, Franklin, and Sebastian Counties, Arkansas. Chicago, IL: Goodspeed Publishing, 1889.

Leflar, Robert A. *The First One Hundred Years: Centennial of the University of Arkansas*. Fayetteville: University of Arkansas Foundation, 1972.

Lemke, Walter J. *Early Colleges and Academies of Washington County*. Fayetteville, AR: Washington County Historical Society, 1954.

Little, Mrs. Anthony George (Hettie). "Noted Daughters of Arkansas." Paper read at meeting of Charlevoix Chapter, DAR, Blytheville, Arkansas, March 1947.

Mahan, Russell L. *The Battle of Fayetteville, Arkansas: April 18, 1863*. Centerville, UT: Historical Enterprises, 1996.

———. *Federal Outpost at Fayetteville: The First Arkansas Union Cavalry*. Centerville, UT: Historical Enterprises, 1996.

Mathews, John Joseph. *Talking to the Moon*. Norman: University of Oklahoma Press, 1945.

Meek, Melinda. "The Life of Archibald Yell." *Arkansas Historical Quarterly* 26, no. 4 (Spring 1967): 353–79.

Members of the Washington County Retired Teachers Association, comps. *School Days, School Days: The History of Education in Washington County.* Fayetteville, AR, 1986.

Methodist Commission on Christian Social Concern. "Report on the Outlook and Attitudes of Negro Young People." This unpublished typed report was the second compiled by the Fayetteville Central Methodist Church's Commission on Christian Social Concern in the spring of 1962. A copy is held by the University of Arkansas Libraries and catalogued as F419 F3 F33.

Neal, Joseph C. *History of Washington County, Arkansas*. Springdale, AR: Shiloh Museum, 1989.

Ormsby, Waterman Lily. *The Butterfield Overland Mail.* 6th ed. Edited by Lyle H. Wright and Josephine M. Bynum. San Marino, CA: Huntington Library, 1968.

Ragland, N.M. "The Arkansas College." Unpublished manuscript. Nathaniel Madison Ragland Papers, 1860–1946, Special Collections, University of Arkansas Libraries, MS R12.

Rhea, J.H. *Thirty Years in Arkansas, and Other Lectures*. Cedar Rapids, IA: Republican Printing Company, 1896.

Thaden, Louise. *High, Wide and Frightened*. Fayetteville: University of Arkansas Press, 2004.

U.S. Fish and Wildlife Service. "The Trail of Tears National Historic Trail and the Tennessee, Wheeler and White River National Wildlife Refuges: Historical and Interpretation Study." Available online at https://www.fws.gov/historicpreservation/publications/pdfs/regionalreports/thetrailoftearsfinalreport.pdf.

Walker, David. *Address of Hon. David Walker, of Fayetteville, Arkansas, on the History and Resources of the State.* Philadelphia, PA: Collins, 1876.

Wappel, Anthony J., and Dennis L. Garrison. *On the Avenue: An Illustrated History of Fayetteville's U.S. Highway 71B*. Fayetteville, AR: Anthony J. Wappel, 2015.

Wappel, Anthony J., and Ethel C. Simpson. *Once Upon Dickson: An Illustrated History, 1868–2000*. Fayetteville, AR: Phoenix International, with the University of Arkansas Libraries Special Collections Department, 2008.

The War of the Rebellion: A Compilation of the Official Records of the Union and Confederate Armies. 128 vols. Washington, D.C.: Government Printing Office, 1880–1901.

Worley, Ted R. "The Story of Alfred W. Arrington." *Arkansas Historical Quarterly* (Winter 1955): 320–22.

Yeater, Sarah J. "My Experiences During the War Between the States." *Arkansas Historical Quarterly* (Spring 1945).

Periodicals

Arkansas Democrat-Gazette. Little Rock, various issues.
Arkansas Gazette. Little Rock, various issues.
Arkansas Historical Quarterly. Fayetteville, Arkansas Historical Association.
Arkansian. Fayetteville, 1859–61.
Fayetteville Democrat. 1860–1932.
Flashback. Fayetteville, AR: Washington County Historical Society, 1951–2016.
Northwest Arkansas Democrat-Gazette. Springdale, various issues.
Northwest Arkansas Times. Fayetteville, 1932–2014.
War Bulletin. Fayetteville, 1862.
Witness. Fayetteville, 1840–41.

INDEX

L

M

N

S

Y

Z

ABOUT THE AUTHOR

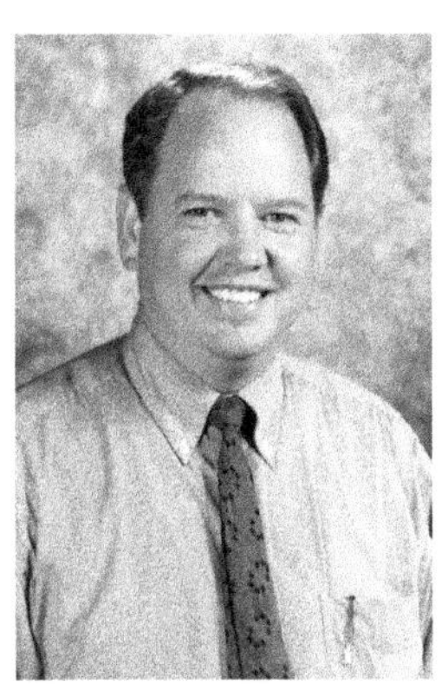

Charlie Alison has lived in Fayetteville since 1965, working as a journalist for the last thirty-five years. He is executive editor for the Office of University Relations at the University of Arkansas, where he edits the alumni magazine and the university's catalogue of studies, among other projects. He is a member of the Washington County Historical Society's board of directors and editor of the society's quarterly historical journal, *Flashback*. He is coauthor with Ellen Compton of *Images of America: Fayetteville*, published by Arcadia Publishing.

Visit us at
www.historypress.net

This title is also available as an e-book